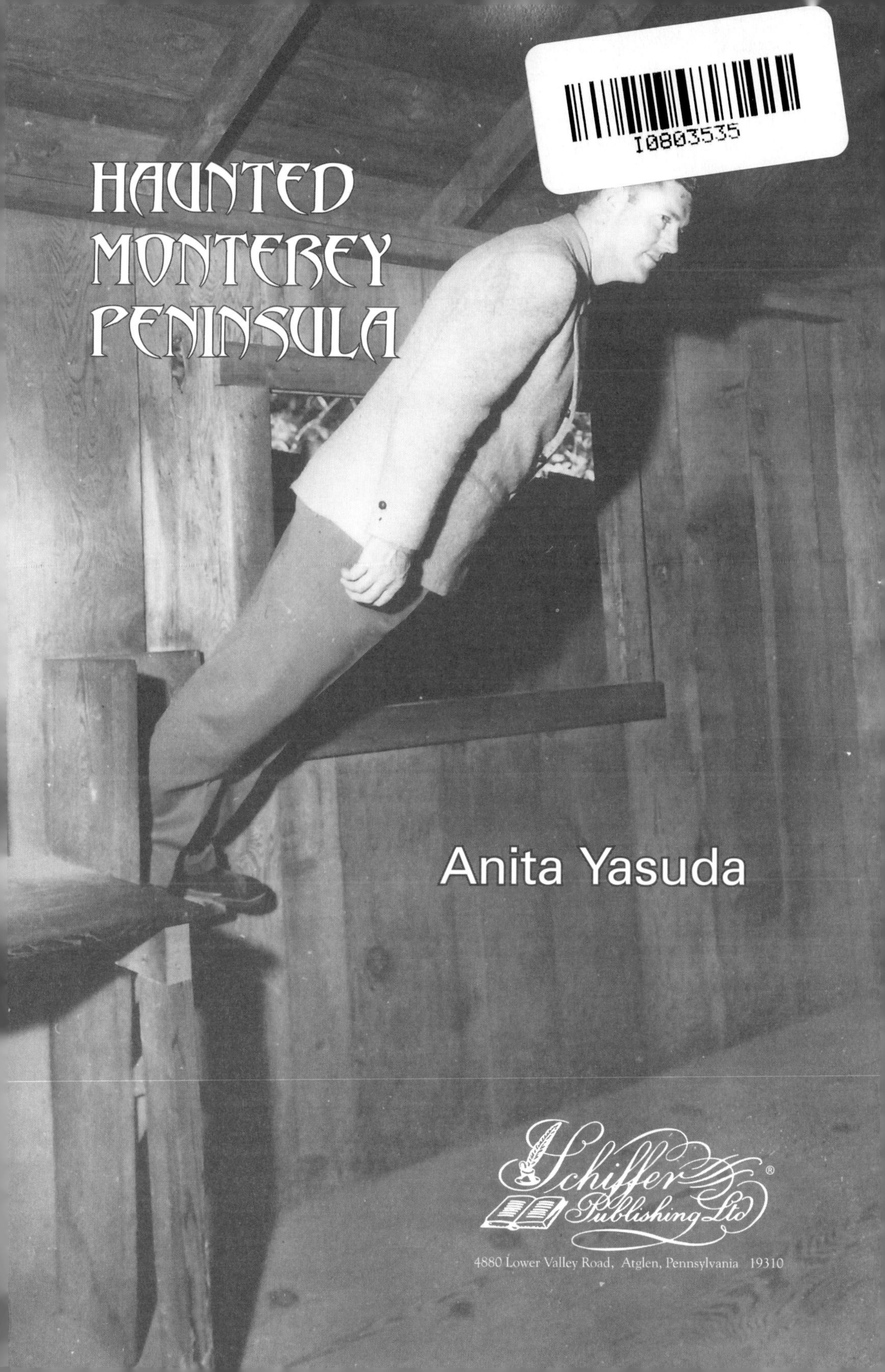

HAUNTED MONTEREY PENINSULA

Anita Yasuda

Schiffer Publishing Ltd

4880 Lower Valley Road, Atglen, Pennsylvania 19310

Other Schiffer Books on Related Subjects:
California Ghosts. Preston E. Dennett. ISBN: 0764319728. $14.95
Ghosts of San Francisco. Kathryn Vercillo. ISBN: 9780764327650. $12.95
Haunts of San Jose. David Lee. ISBN: 9780764330292. $14.99

Published by Schiffer Publishing Ltd.
4880 Lower Valley Road
Atglen, PA 19310
Phone: (610) 593-1777; Fax: (610) 593-2002
E-mail: Info@schifferbooks.com

In Europe, Schiffer books are distributed by
Bushwood Books
6 Marksbury Ave.
Kew Gardens
Surrey TW9 4JF England
Phone: 44 (0) 20 8392-8585; Fax: 44 (0) 20 8392-9876
E-mail: info@bushwoodbooks.co.uk
Website: www.bushwoodbooks.co.uk
Free postage in the U.K., Europe; air mail at cost.

Library of Congress Control Number: 2008937553

Designed by Stephanie Daugherty
Type set in Abaddon™/Zurich BT/Elphinstone™

ISBN: 978-0-7643-3151-0
Printed in in the United States of America

Spring in a Monterey historic garden. The historic Garden League of Monterey is located at 210 Oliver Street.

"There was always something hard to shake off about the ghost story; it is so old and so universal. Our ancestors, as far back as one cares to go, had ghosts. They were, so to speak, part of the household furniture,...and were handed down with the rest of the heirlooms."

~ Robert Leffingwell 1906

Dedication

To Kaylee Emi

Note

This book takes the form of a guidebook to places on the Monterey Peninsula and surrounding area that are associated with ghost stories or supernatural events. The stories are arranged thematically and, wherever appropriate, specific directions are given to locate the "haunting." Sources are listed for all entries. Each entry in the bibliography is keyed to its entry in the body of the book.

**The author took all photography in the book unless noted. The collectible postcards range in value from $4 to $9 U.S.*

Contents

Preface

Ghost stories haunt Monterey's adobe-lined streets. They creep over stones and up adobe walls. Just waiting to be turned over, they lurk under abalone shells. They twist themselves around the mossy trunks of Cypress trees. And on days when thick fog rolls into Monterey Bay, you must might hear from the ghosts themselves.

This is the rich ground from which these legends were born. Not just Monterey but the surrounding Peninsula is full of fascinating stories of pirates, bandits, unrequited love, unsettled spirits, phantom ships, headless riders, and ghosts.

Why is Monterey so different from the rest of California? Perhaps because of its many historic buildings dating back to early California, combined with the fact that three flags once flew over the city – the flags of Spain, Mexico, and the United States. It seems like a foreign city but no border crossing or international flights are required. Around every corner is a story.

A twisted trunk in a Monterey garden.

When I was asked to write this book I jumped at the chance. California is the kind of state that embraces you with her beauty, people, and history. I have spent considerable time in this state and have friends and

Stone wall in the garden of the Larkin House, Monterey, California. The Larkin House was built between 1834 and 1837.

relatives here. It is my second home and one that is never far away. California memories never leave you. Perhaps this is one of the reasons there are so many legends from this state.

Collecting ghost stories is really about an obsession. Like other treasures, they might be battered and bruised with only fragments of names or no names at all connected with the story. To the uninitiated these treasures can look a little suspect. "A ghost story?" someone might ask with just a hint of skepticism in the voice. Better suited to a tabloid headline on the bottom shelf of a supermarket rack that tone suggests.

Closer examination of some stories reveals more about the history of a place and its people, including tragedies, celebrations, and mundane events. Ghost stories are not to be locked up or dusted off for company but rather they are to share with friends or complete strangers. What will eventually become of a collection of ghost stories? As people tell and retell them, they change and develop. For unlike an item, which ends up in a museum, a story will keep on living, for the very telling of it breathes it into life.

Stories

All of the stories presented were researched using historic newspapers, eye witness accounts, and of course first hand experience. You don't have to make a reservation for this tour. Just bring a good pair of shoes, camera, a sense of humor, interest in history, and—last but not least—an open mind.

Rules for Meeting Ghosts

- Remember and respect all private property.
- Obey all entrance rules and time restrictions.
- Just because you are forearmed with information on the type of haunting doesn't always mean you'll meet a ghost.
- Don't be in a rush to finish touring a site or else you will miss the very nuance of a place.

"Sometimes it so happens that a man is allowed to peep over the rim of this materialistic world at things unknown and unknowable into the sphere of shades, the domain of spirits, into the world where reside those who were and now are not-save in shadow."

~ William Alfred Corey 1910

1

Legends of Haunted Shores

Monterey

If there had been a Top Ten Book List in the 1500s, this would have ranked at number one – "*Sergas of Esplandian.*" The book published in 1510 is set on the "fabled" island of California. Yes, California as an island. This fictional point became so widely accepted, some mapmakers drew California as an island. This "small" geographic miss was only the beginning of many misleading points in the story. California was also to the right of the Indies and peopled by Amazons. Okay, so it is a work of fiction and facts certainly can slide a bit, but, for the people of Spain, another aspect of the tale was riveting, the idea that California was a land of abundant riches. And what did they do about it? Why send off an explorer of course. The coffers of the King of Spain could stand to be a little fuller. In 1542 Juan Rodriquez Cabrillo sailed up California's coast in search of riches, but found few.

Sebastien Vizcaino followed much later in his steps and then came Don Gaspar de Portola. Monterey though turned out to be difficult for Portola to find. You might wonder how it could be missed. But this is exactly what happened to Don Gaspar de Portola and Junipero Serra on their first expedition from San Diego in 1769. Sebastian Vizcaino's descriptions of his 1602 voyage were elaborate and also embellished. Comparing the area's climate to that of Seville's is but one example. Monterey's high temperature ranges from around ten degrees Celsius (fifty degrees Fahrenheit) in winter to twenty-four degrees Celsius (seventy-five degrees Fahrenheit) in the summer. Seville in contrast is one of the warmest cities in Europe.

Junipero Serra Monument at the Vizcaino Landing Site. It is here Sabastian Vizcaino planted the Spanish flag and claimed California for Spain.

Just as the explorers began their journey to Monterey by the bay, many tourists do so today. Strolling along Fisherman's Wharf visitors are greeted with colorful candy stores, fish restaurants, whale watching cruise boats, and souvenir shops stocked with postcards and coats for that unpredictable Monterey weather. It is with the weather that our first story begins. The cool and sometimes misty climate of Monterey can take first time visitors to the city by surprise. Monterey is often shrouded in fog, as this first legend explains.

This story made an appearance in a late 1800s issue of *The San Francisco Call*, one of the largest papers on the Pacific coast. The *Call* attracted many talented artists and writers, such as Mark Twain, who worked there from 1863-1864.

Legend of the Fog ~ Monterey

Turning his back on the angry mob on shore the padre vowed never to return to Monterey. Never.

It was the late 1700s and a new padre had come to an equally new mission. This being the mission of Santa Cruz, named for the Holy Cross. Mission Santa Cruz, the twelfth mission in the chain of twenty-one missions in Alta, California, established in 1791, lay at one end of the crescent shaped bay—Monterey Bay.

Looking for guidance from his brethren at the San Carlos Borromeo de Carmelo, the padre set off early one morning. He thought himself well prepared for his new position in Santa Cruz. Hadn't he received letters in Spain detailing the achievements of the Mission? These he was forced to realize were written by someone with an eye on the past and not firmly rooted in the present.

In the first months he had thrown himself into his work. Wheat and corn crops were planted. There was talk of a vineyard and, of course, like the other missions, cattle and sheep were being raised. Though Santa Cruz had flourished for six years, present challenges were rapidly erasing what good had been done, devastating rainstorms, the killing of a priest, forced evacuation of the mission due to a pirate threat, subsequent looting of the mission, and now the establishment of a settlement by the Spanish government. Gamblers and smugglers were in abundance, while converts to Catholicism were not. Seeing the numbers of Indians steadily decreasing, the lures of the pueblo being greater than the mission, the padre increasingly doubted himself. Doubt, he had been instructed since childhood, was a disease. If allowed to grow, doubt impaired God's work.

Cypress trees lining the shore lifted the padre's mood temporarily, bringing to mind memories of Damascus. The padres here could surely advise him. With the shoreline steadily approaching, the padre could see the local Indians. This was certainly a sign of good things to come. He breathed in the cool air, allowing himself to relax.

Without warning, a large rock fell dangerously close to the side of the boat. The padre could now clearly see Indians brandishing weapons. With the recent murder of one of his brethren, the padre gripped the side of the boat a little tighter. Saying a quick prayer he faced the shore – he would meet any challenges God set before him. "Tell them I have to come to visit with my brothers at the mission," he demanded of his guide. The guide quickly complied. This only brought forth more angry gestures. Infuriated, the padre leapt to his feet, almost capsizing the boat. Steadying himself with one hand on his guide and one in the air he proclaimed in a voice that echoed across the bay, "Because you have done this thing,

Monterey shall never show her fairest face to her visitors again." And to this day, whenever strangers fill the town, the wind blows, clouds roll in, and the fog descends.

Tales

There are many versions of this story. Some see the character of the padre replaced by a cold-hearted fortune hunter. The man who has come to find the padre's hidden silver mine is refused entry to the bay. He responds by cursing the town. Whichever version you prefer, it is an interesting tale to think about if visiting Monterey you should find her shrouded in mist.

Location

There are many ways to enjoy Monterey Bay. One is strolling along Fisherman's Wharf located at the end of Alvarado Mall, just off the municipal wharf on Lighthouse Avenue. Walking along the shore by the Customs House, Henry Dana's world so well documented in his book *Two Years Before the Mast* comes to life. It is easy to imagine vessels filled with wine from the East, silks, brocades, wagon wheels, spices, and other stuff unloaded as cargo.

Before you set off in search of the Santa Cruz mission, only a half size replica of The Mission Santa Cruz (*Misson la exaltacio de la Santa Cruz*) exists today. It is California Landmark 342. Earthquakes in 1840 and 1857 destroyed the church. This mission was built in 1931, operates as a museum, and is open to visitors. The Holy Cross Church sits on the original site and has an active parish.

The mission is open from Tuesday to Saturday from 10am until 4pm and Sunday from 10am until 2am. It is closed on holidays. The phone number is (831) 426-5686.

The Black Ship ~ Monterey Bay

Ghostly Snapshot

Can a phantom ship take on new crew members? You might think this is impossible but one vessel sometimes seen off the coast of Monterey does. Just ask John.

Mast of a sailing ship.

A tall ship sails into the harbor. The standard it bears is black, with skull and crossbones. Pirates. Robert Louis Stevenson after his trip to the region may have been inspired to write about pirates and buried treasure in the classic *Treasure Island*.

"Fifteen men on the dead man's chest-Yo-ho-ho, and a bottle of rum!" RLS

Though his pirates were fictional, pirates to Monterey were not. In 1818 Monterey became the only Californian city to be attacked by a pirate ship. The pirate's name was Hippolyte Bouchard and during the Spanish-American wars of independence he sailed into Monterey Bay with the purpose of plundering her. While he didn't find riches, he was successful in terrorizing the area. More about this fascinating man can be found in the book *The Burning of Monterey* by Peter Uhrowczik.

There are over one hundred and forty shipwrecks in the Monterey Bay National Marine Sanctuary and more are undocumented. In an area littered with shipwrecks, one real pirate attack and several lost treasure in Monterey Bay stories, it is little wonder ghost ship legends such as "The Devil's Ship" developed. Fans of gothic literature will also recognize this legend as a version of the Faust myth – "selling one's soul to the devil."

A tall ship sat upon the glassy waters of the bay. "Ship in port," a voice bellowed. The wooden shutter of the lookout banged shut and John scrambled down the ladder. A new ship in port meant there was work to be had. Late into the night one old sailor had entertained John with stories of sailing to the Sandwich Islands and the Orient. John had imagined himself in those far-flung places and now here in Monterey Bay a ship had come into port. What luck. Wherever she was going, John was going. At fourteen he wanted nothing more than to leave his father's farm. "Adventure is it? We'll see you back before a fortnight," his father had scoffed. John quickly dressed, wondering briefly what his parents would say when they found out. His brothers would be angry doing his share of the chores and his mother sad, this was certain. But John's mind was too full of tales of treasure for this to be a deterrent.

The others at the boarding house were sound asleep. Strangely the call had only awakened John. Even more peculiar was the complete absence of Customs House officials by the shore. It was as if the fog that had now rolled into Monterey had cast a spell upon her. As John contemplated what to do next, the form of a man appeared out of the mist. He was dressed in black from head to toe. "Is that your ship?" asked Jack. The man nodded yes. For a moment John forgot why he had come but, quickly recovering his composure, asked about work aboard. "Is it work you're after or riches?" asked the man. John quickly answered, "Why I'd sell my soul to get out of this town." With that he was hired on the spot. "How should I address you sir?" John asked. "Master," the man said simply, turning his back on John and walking back to his small rowboat. Though John could not see the schooner, his new master had no difficulty directing John until they were alongside the majestic black schooner. Unseen hands threw down a rope ladder and up John climbed to his new life.

Back at the boarding house the sailors were just waking up. Some time would pass before they noticed John gone. Later John's father would come into town in search of the boy but by then it would be too late. If the sailor on duty opened the wooden shutter now, he would not see billowing sails as John had, but tatters, a once gleaming haul now full of holes and in the portals faces so lifeless, he would say their very souls had been sucked from their bodies. This ship you see was not an ordinary trading vessel, it was the devil's ship. The only trade it ever did was in souls. Legend had it any man agreeing to work for the "master" would be destined to serve for the next fifty years. As for John, he was never seen again.

Manifestations

Where there is a port city, there are bound to be tales of ghostly pirates and ships that come into port when "conditions" are perfect. On foggy nights go down to the water's edge if you dare, you just might catch a glimpse of the Devil's Ship.

Phantom Ship Lore

In an article from an 1894 issue of *The Fresno Morning* an old salt sums up the ghost ship this way. *"It's the ships that never went out from any port that a sailor never forgets when he sees one of them."* A phantom ship sighting was considered a warning of death.

Location

Customs House is located at 20 Customs House Plaza. The entire area is a charming pedestrian-walk. A fountain, nearby park, and occasional street performer make it a great spot for creating a few new Monterey memories. If Maritime history interests you, the Maritime Museum of Monterey is a stones throw away at 5 Custom House Plaza. The Fresnel lens from the Point Sur lighthouse is one of many intriguing displays. In the days before the wharf was built, ships would drop anchor, then use small boats to row ashore.

Background

Thomas O. Larkin, a prominent figure in Monterey who served as the first and last American Consul, used an existing piece of land north of Custom House for the wharf. In the 1870s the Pacific Coast Steamship Company constructed a wharf at Monterey for regular passenger and freight service. This wharf has seen many expansions and changes from lumber and grain hub to the sardine collapse of the late 1950s, to the tourist destination it is today. If a stranger dressed in black asks you to row him out to his ship, it is best to keep on walking.

"...that phantom ship, whose form shoots like a meteor through the storm; (sic) And well the doomed spectators know 'tis harbinger of wreck and woe."

~ Sir Walter Scott: Rokeby, ii.11.

The Ghost of The Pescadero ~ Pebble Beach

Sometimes time doesn't flow in the direction we usually perceive it to. This phenomenon is called a time slip. Many novels are based upon it, seeing the protagonist embark on a series of time-traveling adventures. They may journey well into the future or deep into the past. Reports of modern day time slip occurrences are usually of the more mundane variety, such as a vision of a street from long ago, the appearance of a person dressed in period clothing who appears momentarily holding the spectator's stare just long enough to create a lasting impression. The following legend from Carmel's Pescadero Canyon is one such example, merging two ghost sightings into a modern day nightmare.

The Pescadero Canyon is a beautiful area. It is seemingly unchanged by time, due in part to strict environmental protection laws, which have recognized it as an environmentally sensitive habitat. The area runs from Highway 1 to the beach. On the opposite side of the canyon is the Del Monte Forest of Monterey County. It is home to towering redwoods, deer, bobcats, and even a ghost legend. It is hard to believe now but once this place of singular beauty was to be avoided in the days preceding Christmas.

Is there a ghost lurking somewhere in this canyon?

The Hunter

In the forests of the Pescadero was a doe and her fawn like no others. One hunter who was unfamiliar with the area went hunting in the Pescadero days before Christmas, unaware of the admonition to avoid doing so. He walked along a cattle trail following the tracks of a doe and a fawn. Around a bend in the track he caught sight of the doe and fired. Down she went. He hurried over but to his amazement she got up, looked at the hunter, and walked off. Certain he had hit her, the hunter went after the doe. The tracks were plain for a couple of miles, but strangely there were no specks of blood or any other indication that the animal had been hurt. Puzzled, the hunter continued his pursuit until he saw the doe and fawn feeding quietly. He raised his rifle to fire again but in the same moment she turned to look at him. The hunter gasped for he no longer saw the face of a deer but that of a woman with her child. Then the images simply vanished. The hunter ran all the way back to his camp and it is said he never hunted there again. As for the woman and her child, it was never determined who they could be.

The Hikers

In a local bar, a group of men who had traveled to the area to hike heard this tale of the unfortunate hunter and laughed. A curse? Riiiiiight. Weren't they the stuff of late night movies or "Brady Bunch" adventures in Hawaii? The bartender explained to the trio again how misfortune would befall those who met the woman and her child during the weeks before Christmas. The hikers were not swayed by the story; they even suggested the bartender had imbibed his own liquor.

The next day the trio set off at a leisurely pace for the canyon. One member of the group, David, had not been able to sleep after hearing the bartender's story. He was not an overly superstitious man but, nevertheless, the story resonated with him. The guys had teased him relentlessly after he suggested they change their plans. Loaded down with camping gear the men made slow progress; when they could continue no more, the group found shelter in a small clearing, where they were rewarded with a great view of Carmel Bay. While David slept soundly, his friends were awakened by the sounds of crying. Straining their eyes to look into the darkness, they saw two forms. Unbelievably it was a woman and a child. The same ones the bartender had warned them about. They could see the images as clearly as if they were watching a film. The hair of the mother clung to her head, matted with blood. On her neck was another wound, from which issued a stream of blood. The child clutched at her hand, locking eyes with the two men the entire time. The visions only lasted for a moment before the Pescadero slipped back into stillness.

The next morning, the men endeavored to explain away the strange occurrences of the night by blaming it on a combination of overactive imagination and too much physical exertion. David, who slept through the night, was overcome with an overwhelming feeling of apprehension. He tried to convince his friends to pack it in early and return home. Before the trio could come to any agreement, one man spotted a ship off shore. It looked to be in distress. After drawing straws, David stayed behind with their belongings.

He watched his friends from the top of a high hill near the camp. They made their way down to the beach where they found a sturdy rowboat, probably belonging to a local fisherman. They pushed it out into the choppy waves. After an hour or more had passed, they had made little progress towards the mystery ship, as the sea was very rough. With fog rolling in and his view now completely obscured David kept a bright fire going, not knowing when they would return. Day turned to night and the next morning when he awoke the ship was gone. Thinking the ship had dropped his friends back in Monterey, David proceeded back alone, leaving the camping gear to be retrieved at a later date. His friends would be back in the bar, having a pint and talking of their short adventure, David reasoned.

But this was not the case. After careful questioning, David was told no boat had been seen. The people in town knew what David was slowly realizing – his friends had embarked on a voyage from which no man ever returned. Proof yet gain of the Pescadero curse. {1}

Location

Pescadero Point is between Stillwater Cove and Crocker Cypress Grove. Mr. and Mrs. Paul Fagan gave the Pescadero Point parcel of land to the Monterey Peninsula Foundation in 1958. Pescadero means fishing place in Spanish. Before the Spanish, the American Indians, Oholones, knew this spot well. Today you can still find hundreds of clam and abalone shell fragments. The landmark cypress, the Witch tree, is located here. The tree is no longer standing but its trunk is roped off. There is no public access to the point.

"In the combined strangeness and monotony of life at sea weird tales spring up naturally. The many freaks of sea and sky, the unexplored coasts and unexplained phenomena which the sailor often meets on his way give food for the imagination..."

~ Hanna Astrup Larsen 1906

The Chinese Fisherman ~ Big Sur & Point Lobos

History

The land of "gum saan or golden mountains" lured many Chinese to California. Conditions on board trading ships, which brought them across the Pacific were extremely hard. The author Joseph Splivalo used his great-uncle's records to describe the voyage:

> Even at its best the trip from China to California in sailing ships must have been miserable. The poor people were herded in the hold of the ship like a flock of sheep, with no sanitation; their food consisted of a rice cooked in water with some pork fat. *[sic]* ...many Chinese emigrants died and were thrown into the sea. If the ship sank during the storm everyone in the hold was drowned.

Point Lobos, now a state park south of Monterey, is considered the first Chinese fishing settlement in California. It is believed Chinese arrived at Point Lobos around 1851. Today a cabin built by Chinese workers is still standing and used as a museum. In national papers of the late 1890s reports surfaced of a dead Chinese fisherman wandering along the rocky shore. The figure of a man dressed in traditional Chinese costume consisting of short black coat, pants, and large bamboo hat covered in seaweed sparked terror in the Chinese fishing community. It doesn't sound all that scary today but it was rumored if you saw him it would be your last moment alive.

Look for the ghost of the abalone fisherman at Point Sur.

The Fisherman

One day a young Chinese fisherman traveled with a group of men from Point Lobos to Point Sur. Here living on the rocky bottom were said to be rich beds of shallow-water abalone just waiting to be harvested. The men were excited at the prospect of a large harvest due to an increasing demand abroad. With the proceeds from the catch one man dreamed of returning to his wife and children in China a wealthy man. For the young man, who was new to the Coast, his dreams were simple. Eager to collect many abalones, he confidently waded into the ocean. Scanning the waters below he could see abalone every foot or so. Unaware that each step was taking him further from his friends, he quickly filled his basket. Calls to him to stay close to shore went unheeded.

The young man couldn't believe his good fortune. Each shell seemed larger than the last. Then out of the corner of his eye he spotted a magnificent abalone. Though Californians were odd in their dislike of eating abalone, the shells were highly prized for jewelry. Why he had sold a shell half this size for a good sum just last week. As he reached for the shell, he felt a sharp tug on his foot. The man spun around and dropped his long wooden pole. The tide quickly carried it from his grasp. Grabbing his leg with both hands, he pulled with all his might, but could not free his leg. It was then that he noticed the inky black water around him. It was blood – his blood. He screamed loudly for his fellow fishermen but they couldn't hear him above the roar of the waves. A slow nauseating feeling crept over the man as he realized he was alone. In a final effort to break free, he again gripped his leg. It was then he realized to his horror that his foot was not wedged in a rock, but in a giant abalone. The monster abalone was slowing crushing his foot.

Finally hearing his cries, the friends raced towards the man but it was too late. They could only watch helplessly as the giant abalone pulled the man under the waves. It didn't help that none of them could swim. Papers reported the friends of the drowned man saying "*[sic]* the ghost of the dead Chinaman had turned into an abalone and would seek other victims until the last of his comrades was dead."

Such was their belief in this that the fishermen turned to ancient superstitions to protect themselves against both the monster of the sea and their friend who had become one. In an effort to rid the area of the man's ghost, the fishermen burned his belongings and clothes. The article ends with the reporter saying, "They (the man's friends) then put a sign in Chinese on the top of the cliff, and as I have heard, no Chinaman has ever since ventured to fish in that cove." {2}

Manifestations

The phantom Chinese fisherman can occasionally be seen wandering amongst the rocks. Some say he is looking for "friends" to take with him far below the ocean's surface. Others speculate he is looking for his severed foot.

Note

It is interesting that a very similar story circulates on Santa Cruz Island. This story appears in *Haunted California* by Barbara Smith and in *Ghosts of the Haunted Coast* by Richard Senate. In both stories the Chinese fisherman loses his hand and not his leg. It becomes stuck in the rocks and he is forced to try and cut it off as the tide comes in. What makes the story from Point Sur so interesting is that this man's unfortunate accident can be proven as it was documented in local papers, as were the sightings of his ghost.

Location

Point Sur National Park is nineteen miles south of Carmel along Highway One. On the Big Sur Chamber of Commerce website are driving directions and links to maps. www.bigsurcalifornia.org. Point Lobos is located three miles south of Carmel on Highway One.

"As if a phantom caress'd me, I thought I was not alone, walking here by the shore;" Leaves of Grass Walt Whitman

What's in a Name?

Rolling, diving, and leaping, the Californian sea lion inspired Spanish sailors long ago when they named this stretch of land. Well, it wasn't actually the movement of these creatures but their sound. The haunting sound of sea lions along the rocky coast of what is present day Carmel would inspire Spanish sailors in the 1600s. It is a honking bark that never seems to stop. They will bark all night long for no apparent reason. Their barking reminded the sailors of wolf howls. And so a rocky stretch of shoreline became known as Punta de Los Lobos Marinos or Point of the Sea Wolves. It is known today simply as Point Lobos.

History

The area is rich in history, being used by the Oholone Indians and much later the Chinese would fish these shores. It is believed the Chinese arrived at Point Lobos around 1851. In Jonathan Kemp's article, "Chinese Start Monterey Fishing Industry," he writes, "Chinese fishermen were the first to mine the rich marine treasures of Monterey Bay, and their industrious efforts helped make Monterey one of California's most successful fishing ports." Chinese fishing camps were located at Point Lobos, Pescadero (now Stillwater Cove), and at Point Alones, now what is Cannery Row. According to Arthur F. McEvoy ("In Places Men Reject Chinese Fishermen at San Diego, 1870-1893," *The Journal of San Diego History*, Fall 1977 Volume 23 Number 4): *"A noteworthy exception to the pattern of restricted opportunity that confronted the Chinese in early California was the fishing industry that developed in the bays and coastal waters near San Francisco, Monterey, and San Diego. There was a lot of room on the ocean: While in other sectors of the state's economy the Chinese sojourners were either forced into subordinate roles or driven out altogether by competing whites, here they were able to pursue their own ends in relative peace*."

Visitors to the area can enjoy a network of trails laid out by Frederick Law Olmstead or explore a cabin built by Chinese workers presently used as a museum. If the following report is true maybe the Chinese never left.

Phantom Village

Another way to view Point Lobos is from the ocean. Whale-watching excursions are popular year round in Monterey, with grey whales migrating during the months of December through to May, followed by other migratory species. A woman (unidentified) reported to the author, Randolph Reinstedt, of *Ghost Notes*, an odd experience while on such a whale-watching excursion. It was during the 1980s and the woman was part of a group on a daytime cruise, which took them past Point Lobos. Standing on the outer deck there was nothing different at first to separate this group from any other. The excursion was preceding as any other with sightings of whales, marine birds, and sea lions, when passengers noticed something not quite right with the coastline. On the farthest tip of the point was a village where one had not been moments before. Astonished, the passengers could not take their eyes from this site, which upon closer inspection resembled a Chinese fishing settlement. What is even more astounding is not just one person saw the village, but everyone on deck did.

There was never a Chinese settlement on the point, but there was one in Whalers Cove. It is interesting to wonder what caused this distortion in time and space. Perhaps, time slips don't just occur in movies with Jane Seymour and the late Christopher Reeve. The movie, by the way, was *Somewhere in Time*.

Haunted Cypress ~ Monterey

Ghostly Snapshot

If the news articles from the 1930s are to be believed, the trees around Monterey are to be feared. Evil lurks around their twisted limbs waiting for unsuspecting passersby.

A Monterey Cypress tree near the village of Carmel.

It's easy to seek out specters and spirits around Monterey Bay. They haunt historic homes, churches, hotels, and even trees. Trees? Yes, even trees. The following poem "Neath Monterey Pines" was written by Grace Hibbard around 190? – exact date unknown. Here are just a few lines from the piece in which the author successfully sums up what people claimed to have heard in cypress groves.

"Neath Monterey Pines"

"There are voices in the pine trees,
Voices soft and low-
Listen, listen to the message
Hearts their own will know"

From the late 1800s to 1920, stories of the Monterey cypress's otherworldly properties flourished (no pun intended) in newspapers. Reporters used words such as "giant, misshapen, and leafless" to describe the trees, which in all fairness must have seemed right out of a horror novel to some journalists used to the landscape of the Eastern seaboard. Now you might think that many trees lose their leaves, they are called deciduous and if you looked out of your window you might see a few. But to these journalists there just had to be a supernatural explanation for the bent and gnarled form of the cypress. It surely could not just be due to the Westerlies, the wind that sweeps in from the Pacific.

Supernatural

Locals did little to dissuade visitors from thinking the trees were supernatural. Quite to the contrary, some guides emphasized the odd to entice visitors to come and see first hand the local scenery. In a 1875 handbook to Monterey, the trees are described as "*[sic]* silent as the Pyramids, mystical as the Sphinx, the gnarled gray trunks supporting the golden green branches a fit haunt for departed spirits, a Merlin, or a slumbering cot for a child of Cain."

Authors such as Robert Louis Stevenson also found inspiration in the cypress with its odd looking branches sculpted by the wind. He described them as "ghosts fleeing before the wind." The first fifteen chapters of *Treasure Island* may have been written at Braemar, Scotland, in 1881, but local legend has it he used Point Cypress as the locale of Spyglass Hill.

In 1894 a New Jersey newspaperman had this to say about his trip to Monterey. "The trees are gnarled and twisted into various shapes, and their flat tops give them the form of an immense umbrella. This is the only place where they are known to exist. Dante, in writing his 'Inferno', must have dreamed of the Monterey cypress." (Parkinson, Edward S. *Wonderland or 12 weeks in and out of the United States.* (Trenton, NJ: MacCrellish & Quigley, 1894)).

Bad Reputation

The bad reputation of these trees was not only due to their unusual looks, but also owing to their uncanny noises. They are said to be groaning souls in distress. If that was not enough to warrant labeling the trees evil, then the notion the trees attracting the dead surely was. "That it (the cypress) leans always toward the ocean and is quite commonly seen with its lower limbs hung with dead serpents and other crawling things that have come up from the water is another fact cited by those who credit the tree with little good," wrote one reporter. "It is said by those who know it (the cypress) well to be haunted, a menace to the good fortune of all who pass within its radius." The trees were so haunted in fact misfortune could come your way merely by passing too close to these giants, not that any specifics were ever given. {3, 4}

Tree Spirits

Maybe the tales surrounding the cypress are linked to both native and European myths. Stories of tree spirits are quite common around the world. In the fifteenth century, Europeans believed that evil spirits lived in forests where men went to hunt. If men failed to return from a hunt, evil wood spirits were blamed. They also believed that the trees maintained the most powerful of all spirits and that these spirits were good. Before entering a forest they would knock on the wood to awaken the spirit to protect them. This is where the saying "knock on wood" comes from.

Legends of tree spirits closer to home also exist. Katherine Berry Judson, author of *Myths and Legends of California and the Old Southwest,* writes of the redwoods. The large redwood trees near Kern River in California were sacred to the Monos who called them "woh-woh-nau," an onomatopoeic word meant to sound like an owl. The owl was the guardian spirit of the trees. Legend had it if the tree was cut down you would bring bad luck upon yourself.

There are no reports in recent years of either possessed trees or people being cursed by walking near them. Where reporters in the past saw evil in the Monterey Cypress, it is pretty safe to say that any reports surfacing today are on the beauty and rarity of this species of Cypress. But with a good strong wind, a misty night, and a healthy imagination the Cypress could still find its way into a ghost story.

What's in a Name?

Some Monterey Cypress trees were given appropriate eerie sounding names such as the Ghost Tree or the Witch Tree. The Ghost Tree is said to awaken when waves swell off shore. A journalist writing in *Sunset Magazine* had this to say, "The Old Witch tree, among the ancient cypress along the famous 17-Mile Drive, at Monterey, is the symbol of the enchantment that holds this region of surpassing beauty. (February 1914 p. 298) The image of many turn of the twentieth century postcards, today the Witch

Tree is no longer standing, with only the trunk still visible but roped off at Pescadero Point.

Mysterious Origins

The mysterious origins of the cypress may have something to do with the tree's bad reputation. In one version traveling monks from the Buddhist monastery at Lhasa sailed across the Pacific Ocean. They marked this voyage by planting seeds from the sacred trees. Others say the cypress grew from seeds, which drifted long ago across the Pacific from Japan.

Location

Cypress Point is the major promontory between Monterey and Carmel Bays. The Cypress Point lookout is located along 17-Mile Drive. The famous road winds its way between palatial homes, some more modest ones are set well back in the trees, a spectacular coastline, world famous golf courses, and of course the last remaining forest of that rare species of tree, the Monterey Cypress. The lookout provides a great view of the Pacific coastline. The Ghost Tree breaks at Pescadero Point, at the northern edge of the 18th hole at Pebble Beach Gold Links, on 17-Mile Drive in Pebble Beach.

Ferguson's Ghost ~ Pebble Beach

Ghostly Snapshot

Could a man be responsible for the twisted cypress? And could his spirit still be lurking near one of the most famous trees in Pebble Beach? The White Lady ghost of Pebble Beach may have a friend in the shape of an old sailor called Ferguson who liked to tell tall tales.

Ferguson

Ferguson worked on ships his entire life. Why he would say his feet would turn to bricks if he stayed on land too long. But one year when his whaling boat docked in Monterey, Ferguson didn't return to it. No, he stayed on shore and watched as

The Royal Presidio Chapel of Monterey, California.

The Royal Presidio Chapel of Monterey, California.

the boat sailed out of sight. It hadn't been something he planned on – deserting ship and all. But when he set foot in Monterey his feet didn't turn into bricks and, if anything, his stride became longer and his chest a little prouder. He settled himself at a local saloon and found an audience for his sea tales. As the days wore on his tales got longer and longer – for example, he told of slaying a shark in Panama with only a knife. The next time you heard that story he might have slain two sharks or more. And how about the time he killed a whale with only his bare hands and some said a dragon. The dragon bones he cut up and placed in the sidewalk outside of the Presidio Chapel. But the tallest tale Ferguson told was how he tied knots in the Monterey cypress trees.

There were many skeptical of these claims, but as Ferguson was truly a brave and strong man who wrestled bears and bulls behind Pacific House, no one minded his tales. He was further welcomed into the community when he married a local girl by the name of Senora Estrada. Instead of wrestling bears and bulls, Ferguson could be seen fetching and carrying whatever his wife demanded. After a year of marriage, Ferguson began to feel quite badly at his deception, as his wife, you see, truly believed those tales.

One day Ferguson confessed to his wife he had never slain a dragon or a shark or even a whale. He had in fact been the ship's cook. Senora Estrada didn't know what to make of his confession. It didn't seem possible that he could have deceived her, for there in front of the Presidio Chapel was indeed a sidewalk made of dragon bone. No, Ferguson told her, they were whalebones. Senora Estrada's eyes sparkled with wonder. Oh what an amazing husband he was. In the middle of the night he transformed the sidewalk into whalebone. If he was capable of such feats then he should go right away and straighten out the cypress tress. Ferguson begged his wife to understand it was not he, but she wouldn't hear of it. She instructed him to straighten out every tree and not to return home until he had.

Ferguson, glumly packed up his few possessions and set out for the cypress forest. And there he lived for the rest of his life. He became such a well-known hermit that when the writers and artists moved into the Carmel area they often sought him out. Ferguson couldn't fix trees but he could tell a tall tale.

Manifestations

It is said Ferguson's spirit still lingers in the cypress groves of Pebble Beach. If you stand very still and listen, sometimes you will hear Ferguson telling a long-long tale. The Ghost Tree on 17-Mile Drive is where the ghost of Ferguson lingers. *

~ Source – George W. Caldwell.

"Whatever hour you woke there was a door shuting. From room to room they went, hand in hand, lifting here, opening there, making sure – a ghostly couple."

~ A Haunted House, Virginia Woolf

2

Cryptozoology

Introduction

Watch the grainy video – it's a bird, it's a plane, no it's an unidentified animal. Welcome to the world of Cryptozoology, the study of animals that have not yet been verified. These are elusive creatures, usually relegated to myths, B movies or homemade video. With the discovery of or rediscovery of animals such as the giant squid, a creature so infrequently seen that scientists once questioned its very existence, the search for more cryptoids is hotter than ever.

Before you dismiss this as pseudo science, in 2005 the Global Underwater Search Team of Sweden started the world's first school for cryptozoologists. One of their members, Jan Sundberg, during a 2004 interview with Stephen Pincock from *The Scientist*, summed up his motivation this way, "But when you spend so long doing something like this, you start to believe in it," he says. "Now, when scientists tell me there's nothing in that lake, I think [that] they're wrong, and I'm going to prove they're wrong."

Where else do cryptozoologists find inspiration? Why, in discoveries of new animals, some made as recently as one hundred years ago. Though P.T. Barnum's mermaid was a hoax, it is interesting to note the gorilla wasn't discovered until 1847, the giant panda not seen alive until 1936, and the coelacanth thought to be extinct for millions of years until it was caught off the coast of South Africa in 1938.

In a time when it seems there are not many more places to explore, it is interesting to note that less than five percent of the ocean has been explored. With new technologies, we know a lot more about the ocean today, but that doesn't mean it isn't without a fright or two. Maybe there *is* something lurking off the coast of Monterey. Is it Nessie's cousin?

The Old Man ~ Monterey

"The sailor as a class still holds fast to the superstitions that have been his especial heritage throughout all ages. To him the sea is still peopled with phantoms."

~ 1907, author unknown

Eyewitnesses report seeing a sea monster—it's part human and part fish! Some people think the monster may be the descendent of a plesiosaur. But others think it is just myth. "The greatest difficulty in obtaining evidence in regard to the sea serpent is the ridicule with which its publication is greeted. Naturalists have been far less incredulous than the general public," Professor Proctor – English scientist, *The Washington Times,* April 24, 1904.

Visitors to the Monterey Aquarium stand in wonder in front of one of the main exhibits, a three-story 335,000-gallon tank with clear acrylic walls that offer a stunning view of leopard sharks,

A view of the Pacific Ocean.

sardines, anchovies, and other sea creatures swimming through a towering kelp forest. Children run straight into the exhibit (literally), pressing noses and hands against the case. There are oohs and ahs in a multitude of language. But the creature that has had Monterey talking for years does not reside within these acrylic walls. No, it lies somewhere off the Monterey coast and between the 1930s and 1940s it was often spotted. The creature is none other than "The Old Man of Monterey" or "Bobo." Yes, the peninsula has its very own version of the Loch Ness Monster.

Moore's Beach Monster ~ Santa Cruz

Surf boards, funfair attractions, and sea monsters? After the beaching of an unusual animal in 1925 on Moore's Beach in Santa Cruz, now known as Natural Bridges State Beach, sea monster mania hit the Coast. In 1925 on a remote beach just two miles from Santa Cruz a large animal washed shore. What was this unusual creature? Certainly no one had ever seen anything like it before. It just had to be a sea serpent, or did it?

The Moore's Beach creature was described as having a twenty-foot-long neck. Though some scientists thought it was a rare beaked whale or shark, a renowned naturalist and former president of the Natural History Society of British Columbia, E.L. Wallace concluded that the creature was neither. It was a type of plesiosaur, a large marine reptile held over from the Jurassic period. He is quoted as saying, "My examination of the monster was quite thorough. I felt in its mouth and found it had no teeth. Its head is large and its neck fully twenty feet long. The body is weak and the tail is only three feet in length from the end of the backbone of a whale is far larger than any bone in this animal. Again, its tail is too weak for an animal of the deep and does away with that last version. *[sic]* With a bill like it possesses, it must have lived on herbage *[sic]* I would call it a type of plesiosaurus."

There is no definitive conclusion on this one, though Internet speculation has garnered almost as much attention as the "Roswell" cases. It is interesting to note that once thought extinct creatures such as a coelacanth were rediscovered in the twentieth century. A coelanth (see-la-kanth) is five-feet long (1.5 meter) and thought to be extinct until fishermen in the Indian Ocean caught one in 1938. Experts believed the fish was extinct for at least sixty-six million years. This fish looks the same as it did three hundred and forty million years ago, long before many famous dinosaurs were around.

If such a fish, nicknamed a "living fossil," is still around, who knows what else may be lurking off the rocky shoreline of Santa Cruz. Through your binoculars that small dark head just may not be another sea otter but...

Location

Natural Bridges State Beach is at the west end of W. Cliff Drive. Complete directions are available on the California State Parks website at www.parks.ca.gov

"Lots of things happen at sea that you can't explain [sic],... It may be all very well on land to say that there are no ghosts, perhaps there are none there, but you can't tell me that there are not mysterious powers and spirits on the sea."

~ Hanna Astrup Larsen, 1907

What's In The Water? ~ Pacific Grove

From the early 1900s, peaking in the 1940s, sea serpent sightings were at an all time high. Legends of a mysterious, snakelike creature grew by the day. An article from the early 1900s *San Francisco Call* sums it up well with the headline, "The Sea Serpent is a Fact."

"Many of the supposed sea serpents are whales, lines of birds or patches of seaweed, but it is the consensus of opinion among conservative naturalists that these is some gigantic animal in the deep sea yet unknown to science which occasionally comes to the surface showing portions of its form."

With public interest at an all time high, sightings of the serpent who was named "the old man of Monterey Bay" and "Bobo" by the press continued. Just ten years from when the Moore's Beach monster washed ashore came a fresh sighting. This report was printed in the *Oakland Tribune*. The year was 1935, and a man named William Crabbe, the district manager of the Pacific Gas and Electric Company, was spending a spring day at Pacific Grove with his family. Certainly there was nothing odd about that fact but what happened next would force him from his comfortable thoughts into the unknown and then into denial.

This respected man admitted to seeing something out of the ordinary but was reluctant to call it a monster. Perhaps due to his position in the community he didn't want to speculate about a creature others would call a sea monster. He told reporters that the alleged sea serpent spotted by others along the shore was nothing more than "a group of sea lions playing *[sic]*" J.H. McAlphine, manager of the Del Monte Hotel, disagreed heartily with Mr. Crabbe. He told reporters, how could anyone think the creature was a sea lion. What an absurd thing to suggest. It was as obvious as the nose on his face the crowd at Pacific Grove had seen a sea serpent.

Beach Drive, Santa Cruz, c. 1900s, collectible postcard. Produced by Pacific Novelty Co., San Francisco & Los Angeles.

The Pet Theory

The manager used this opportunity to put forth his own theory. Mr. McAlphine claimed he discovered a mysterious trail leading from the Hotel Del Monte. And it was his opinion it was that of a sea serpent! McAlphine was not shy with the media like Mr. Crabbe and embraced the opportunity to outline his pet theory in detail. Highlights of his theory included: it takes four years for a sea serpent to mature and during that time it lies in the mud under the water waiting for the return of its parents. As for scientific proof to back up his theory, Mr. McAlphine offered none but his own two eyes. Who needed scientists when there is a curious hotel manager around?

Mr. McAlphine didn't stop there, he went on to say he became interested in sea serpents back in May 1927 when he was in charge of the Del Monte bathhouse. At that time several bathers reported seeing a peculiar trail leading from the beach to Del Monte. He investigated and found a two-foot wide trail leading from the beach to the lake below the hotel. Soon after a strange monster was cast upon the beach in Santa Cruz. Mr. McAlphine was referring to the Moore Beach monster. Unfortunately his dates don't correlate with the Moore's Beach Monster recorded in the *Santa Cruz Sentinel*. It washed ashore a full two years before he saw his mysterious trail. Mr. McAlphine discovered another trail by the hotel in May 1931 and found it identical to the one in 1927. Right before the sighting at Pacific Grove he discovered the same trail! Surely there was a connection.

The journalist, highly skeptical, asked why there couldn't be a natural explanation? This was the famed Hotel Del Monte after all. Would it be that hard to presume a guest had simply dragged a heavy object, chairs, etc., down to the water's edge? Or perhaps a staff member dragged an ice cooler with beverages for guests? So, if we are to believe Mr. McAlphine the Santa Cruz sea monster actually grew up right by the Hotel Del Monte!

Unfortunately for Mr. McAlphine, the established thought of the day was sea serpents were nothing more than summer resort delusions. The "sea serpent" was a myth used in "fake" advertising for many summer resorts. Being an employee of a resort, he certainly had an upward battle in making his theories believed.

A Sea Serpent by Any Other Name Would be a Bobo?

Citizens of Monterey would have to wait another four years for a sea serpent sighting. It was August of 1939 when Captain Sal Colletto of the ship *Dante Alighieri* and his crew caught sight of the creature. The story was aptly titled, "California Sea Serpent Is Seen Again." Captain Sal Colletto claimed to have seen the creature three times in the past thirty years, but his crew had always doubted him. They had ribbed the captain about his glimpses of a "frightful human face and ghostly fish's body thirty feet long."

The seiner, a small salmon fishing boat, was an hour from Moss Landing, a fishing village on the pivot point of Monterey Bay. The cook, Dominic Costanza, taking a break on deck, was more than a little tired and looking forward to a quick nap and some sun. As he looked out over the glassy water, an object in the water caught his eye. The cook watched speechless as a great head and neck lifted out of the water. "*[sic]* a huge and bloated human face, four feet wide, sticking out of the water without a ripple, apparently taking a nap. The body, smooth and serpentine, was pitch black." Unintentionally humorous, the cook explained to the reporter that at first he thought it was "something he ate" that was causing him to see things.

Costanza regaining his composure quickly yelled for the other members of the crew to come and look at the creature before it lowered its "slippery head and slipped back into the dark waters." The other members of the *Dante Alighieri* were equally spell bound by what they saw. After years of teasing their captain over "the old man of Monterey," with shocked horror they realized that he hadn't been making up any tales. This was the Old Man of Monterey.

The cook later described the monster. "It had a very old man's face or monkey's face, with eyes twice as broad as breakfast buns and a mouth like a crescent moon. Barnacles all over the head, and also along the black body. Folds of white skin hung beneath the neck. The body was as big around as a truck. It must have weighed maybe eight or more tons."

After watching the creature for some time, it slipped quietly back into the bay. It is interesting to note the place where the creature was spotted just off Moss Landing, is where the underwater Monterey Canyon begins.

Say Cheese

The Moss Landing sighting of Bobo caused a renewed rivalry between fishermen on the Peninsula to take the first photo of the creature. Some intrepid souls even went so far as to boast that they had plans to lasso it and bring it to shore. But the crew of the *Dante Alighieri* wanted no part in the race to capture Bobo. One sighting it would seem was more than enough for them. The general consensus of the crew was it would be bad luck to take a photo of the creature. The captain is quoted as saying, "*[sic]* he didn't need a black box to prove his eyes were keen."

There were those of his crew who believed the creature could never be caught on film. "Like the Ghost Dancers of Indo-China who were photographed by an intrepid British explorer and who didn't show up in pictures." Of course, there was one dissenter (name never printed) in the group who wanted to meet Bobo again. He had plans to write to a major Hollywood studio in the hope of borrowing one of their professional movie cameras. He thought Bobo would make a great adventure movie. Though the camera was never lent, the Old Man of Monterey Bay did find his way onto the screen years later. {5, 6, 7, 8, 9}

The Canyon

The deep-sea canyon of Monterey Bay is estimated to be two-miles deep. In an article on deep-sea ecosystems by Laura Tangley for *National Wildlife* (October 1, 2001), she writes there are millions of species, most of them still unidentified by science. "The deep ocean is home to species diversity much, much higher than any of us imagined," says marine biologist and deep-sea explorer Robert Hessler of the Scripps Institution of Oceanography in California. Who knows what exactly lives on the floor of the Monterey Canyon.

The Scientists

How did scientists of the day react to the crew's reports? Not surprisingly, scientists quickly dismissed the crew's report. In the newspaper, *The San Antonio Light*, August 20, 1939, it was reported, "Scientists believe that the fishermen are fatigued and hallucinating and that the creature is driftwood." The public would have to be content with this theory.

It would take a Monterey fisherman by the name of Emo Pieracol to stir up debate again one year later. Twenty-year-old fisherman, Emo Pieracol (name also appeared as Pieracoi in several papers) reported seeing the monster. In an article entitle "Looks Down the Throat of 'Sea Monster'," Emo Pieracol said "*[sic]* he had looked down the throat of 'The Old Man of Monterey Bay', and found 'the old man' stunning." What is very interesting is he encountered the animal in the same spot as the crew of the *Dante Alighieri*.

Pieracol was enjoying a day of fishing just five miles off Moss Landing when he encountered the "monster." In very un-monster-like fashion, the creature was sunning itself on top of the water. "When my boat aroused him," Pieracol said, "he opened his mouth, and it was red inside. He had a head like a hippopotamus, a round bell-like body, which tapered off to a grayish brown color, with ridges of fat down the side of his body. He had giant fins, which protruded three feet from his body. This report was published in various papers, including *The Amarillo News-Globe,* May 12, 1940.

Heebie-jeebies

Less than a year later this headline blared from *The Hayward Review*, "Sea Monster Reappears At Monterey," September 18, 1941, "Gives fishermen acute attack of heebie-jeebies." Two men, Robbie Canepa and Mario Stagnaro, were out fishing for albacore when they spotted an odd shape in the water. Upon further inspection they were shocked to discover the "Old Man" sunning himself twelve miles off Santa Cruz. Overcome with fear, the pair did not stay around to observe the creature. "They had no desire to tangle with the forty-foot monster as their boat was heavily laden." The beast was described as having a head which "*[sic]* resembles a baboon and who flourishes a horn on his tail." The two men raced back to shore and could provide the newspaper with no further details of their short encounter.

A mere eight years later, in 1949, yet another story appeared in *The Charleroi Mail*. Monterey Bay was again filled with monsters. A sea serpent was frightening many Monterey Bay fishermen by surfacing beside their small boats. Later, these reports turned out to be a hoax when the serpent was identified as an elephant seal. Identification was made by Hopkins marine station – when a 17.5 foot long elephant seal washed up on the beach near Fort Ord. Elephant seals possess a small trunk, have teeth up to eight inches long, and faces frequently coated with barnacles.

Before fishermen could be reassured by this finding the next headline appeared on October 19, 1950, "Sea Monster Appears Again." William J. Marchant and two companions reported seeing the "Old Man of Monterey Bay" surface about ten miles out in the Pacific Ocean from the Santa Cruz wharf. These men did not study the animal nor did they attempt to take a photo, instead they admitted to firing five or six shots at the creature until it disappeared underwater. The monster was described as having the "face of a monkey, the shape of a barrel, and being covered completely with hair like a horse." The reporter ends by saying while no one has ever photographed the sea serpent, descriptions of the monster over the ten-year period are identical. This last word is puzzling at best because by now we have descriptions of sea lions, elephants, hippopotamus, horses, barrels, and monkeys!

Though no recent reports have surfaced of Bobo, it is interesting how many new species of animals are being discovered with further scientific exploration of the Monterey Canyon, a submarine canyon beginning at Moss Landing and extending out ninety-five miles into the Pacific Ocean. Three times deeper than the Grand Canyon, it is one of the nation's largest underwater canyons. A channel at least two or three miles deep runs seventy miles out to sea from Moss Landing where Bobo was sighted near Santa Cruz. Is a mysterious yet undiscovered creature lurking there?

The Small Screen

The tale of Bobo inspired films and TV shows such as the 1960s classic "The Wild Wild West". In one episode a sea serpent terrorizing Portuguese fishermen becomes the object of an investigation by agents James West played by Robert Conrad and Artemus Gordon played by Ross Martin. What's not to love about a show featuring a gunslinger, gadgeteer, and a sea monster?

Location

Monterey Bay Aquarium, 886 Cannery Row or see their website for detailed directions www.mbayaq.org There are no "shy sea monsters" lurking at the aquarium but many amazing sea creatures can be seen.

Moss Landing is a short distance from the Monterey Peninsula. See the official Chamber of Commerce website at www.mosslanding.com for more details. Or telephone (831) 633-4501

"But that same image we ourselves see in all rivers and oceans. It is the image of the ungraspable phantom of life; and this is the key to it all."

~ Herman Melville, Moby Dick

The Window ~ The Santa Lucia Mountains

Ghostly Snapshot

Incredible scenery with jaw dropping vistas draw hikers to the Santa Lucias. Occasionally those hikes lead to a special window to another dimension.

Ventana

One of the most beautiful coastal regions in the world is home to the Santa Lucia Mountains. They stretch from Carmel to just north of San Luis Obispo. Some of this range is part of the Los Padres National Forest. Inland from the Big Sur coastline they flank the Ventana Wilderness, named for the Spanish word "window." It is said that this "window to the West" formed the gateway for spirits of the natives entering and departing the physical realm.

The Santa Lucias are also home to another legend concerning the window. If stories are true, there is a tremendous amount of gold in the mountains just waiting to be found. If you think your odds at playing the lottery are better than finding this treasure you might be correct. The Spanish supposedly left the treasure behind. Why they would leave such a valuable treasure behind is just one aspect of the story that treasure seekers brush over.

Sadly, the Spanish didn't leave a map but they did leave one valuable clue. Look through the Ventana, seekers were told, and the location of the gold would be revealed. Now this may have been correct when an enormous slab of rock formed a bridge, thus connecting the Ventana Double Cone, but it collapsed long ago. There are those who doubt the bridge even existed and suggest the Spanish were simply inspired to call this area Ventana after a legend they heard from the Native Indians or were inspired by window-like cutouts along the Big Sur Coast.

Trivia

If you were ever a Nancy Drew fan, then you might remember Nancy and the gang drove her blue Mustang up the coastal highway to Big Sur and the Santa Lucias. "They could see for miles in all directions. Behind them, the tree-covered Santa Lucia Mountains stretched toward the sky. Ahead, the sea glittered white in the late afternoon sun. Around them, the golden hills and dark canyons of Opa led to the rocky cliffs that plunged down to the Pacific Ocean." The story was called *Nancy Drew: The Legend of The Lost Gold Nancy Drew #138*. Nancy, George, and Bess were on the "trail of a dangerous fortune."

"If a 'ghost' is seen hovering about a grave it is the etheric body or shell of a newly buried person."

~ AHT 1908

The Dark Watchers ~ The Santa Lucia Mountains

Ghostly Snapshot

Somewhere near the summit of the Santa Lucias lurk strange and mysterious beings called the Dark Watchers. What better place than a range of mountains seemingly at the top of the world for a mysterious people to inhabit? It is a place of legends rooted in the first native inhabitants of these mountains.

The Chumash

The Chumash Indians may have captured their likeness in cave paintings. The Chumash rock paintings were probably made for religious reasons but archeologists can only guess at the significance of the images. The Painted Cave State Historic Park near Santa Barbara is open to the public. The Chumash believed this site was sacred, perhaps due to echoing in the cave, which they interpreted as spirit voices. Dr. John Johnson,

The setting sun in the hills of Southern California.

curator of anthropology at the Santa Barbara Museum of Natural History, is recorded as saying on a California State Parks Video Transcript – a Tour of Chumash Painted Cave State Historic Park, " Some of the figures are obviously not representing anything in the visible world. They're representing or depicting figures in the supernatural world. *[sic]*" The native interpreter on the same transcript suggested centipede looking figures represented "boats carrying the dead to the islands so their spirits may pass." Are the "Dark Watchers" connected to the Ventana? One possible theory is they are a form of spiritual guide whose purpose is to help souls into the next life.

Just What Do These Creatures Look Like?

Often seen at dusk, the dark watchers have never been known to interact with anyone. They simply appear, as if the mountain air suddenly solidifies in one spot. Never seen during daylight hours, the dark watchers only show themselves at dusk. Their shape has spooked hikers for years.

Literary References

Whatever they may be, the Dark Watchers have inspired writers and poets. The poet Robinson Jeffers wrote of "forms that look human ... but certainly not human" in his 1937 poem, "Such Counsels You Gave to Me." For more on Robinson Jeffers you can visit his landmark home in Carmel, Tor House, which is open to the public on docent led tours. See www.torhouse.org. John Steinbeck in his story "Flight" writes of his character Pepe, "Once on a white barren spur, he saw a black figure for a moment; but he looked quickly away, for it was one of the dark watchers. No one knew who the watchers were, nor where they lived, but it was better to ignore ..." Why it was better to ignore them and pretend you didn't seem them was never discussed. Another interesting story note is shortly before Pepe's glimpse of these creatures he appears as a "grey indefinite shadow merging into the mountainside" to his mother watching from below.

Eyewitness Accounts

An interesting account of the watchers comes from a woman who remembers hiking with her father when she was quite young.

A strange form appeared suddenly on a rocky ledge in front of them. Her father wasted no time in scooping up the girl and hurrying back down the trail. They never spoke about the incident again but she often wondered if this shape was the Dark Watcher. In *Weird California*, the authors write of a high school principal who encountered a figure with a long cape standing on a rock across a canyon only to see it vanish moments later.

Around The World

The Dark Watchers are not just limited to the Santa Lucia Mountains. Around the world there are many reports of fog-like giants living amongst the ridges of mountains. They aren't completely harmless; many climbers have become so spooked in Germany's Hartz Mountains for example that they have fallen to their death. One scientific theory suggests the sky and topography can combine in such a way that the sun projects the shadow of the viewer on clouds or fog several times larger than his or her real size. The shadow looks like a three-dimensional creature but it isn't. Though this explains fog-like images, it certainly doesn't explain the principal's vision dressed in a long cape.

Location

The Santa Lucia Mountains are accessed by numerous trailheads, either from the west off Hwy 1 or on the east from the Salinas or Carmel Valleys. The Chumash Painted Cave is a State Historic Park and directions are available from the California State Parks website. The cave is open dawn to dusk and according to the website is found in a steep canyon above Santa Barbara.

"It was a stately mansion of bygone days, somewhat gloomy looking compared with its modern neighbors. Nobody stayed in it very long and there were blood-curdling tales of the 'doins' of the 'imps of darkness' 'In the dead of the night'."

~ Newspaper report, author unknown, 1900

3

Romantic Legends

The Sherman Rose ~ Monterey

Ghostly Snapshot

According to legend, Lt. Sherman fell in love with a beautiful resident of Monterey, Senorita Bonifacio. The two enjoyed spending time in her garden, but sadly their time was cut short when he was called away. As a token of their affection they planted

White roses by the Sherman Headquarters in Monterey, California. The home is located on Calle Principal.

a rose bush outside of her adobe. When the bush bloomed the Lieutenant said he would return to make her his bride.

Tourists

Those familiar with Civil War history will know then Lt. Sherman never returned to Monterey but that didn't stop a "cottage industry" from growing up around this tale. Local girls would pose as "the lady of Monterey" for twenty-five cents. The real Senorita Bonifacio welcomed many people from around the world to her small adobe. One reporter wrote, "Travelers would remark on the austerity of her adobe. No rich furnishings nor gaudy hangings, a picture of the pope and a scrapbook with letters and calling cards from around the world."

The Haunting

As the years drifted by it was said you could hear the long dead lady's voice coming from the garden and even the sound of strings being plucked. Some romantics claimed the Senorita herself came to her garden at night when the rose was in bloom.

If Senorita Bonifacio did return to her garden there is little sign of her today. The adobe was moved to make way for a bank. A white historical placard in front of the red awning of Community Bank is all that is left. When the adobe was moved a local reporter wrote, "...*[sic]* modern business conditions will erase the last mute evidence of a love-story that is deathless."

The Wall

A part of the adobe wall and the rose was sold to Josephine Mildred Blanch, an artist originally from Texas who lived in a cottage between Del Monte and Monterey. She was a member of the Pacific Coast Women's Press Association. She remained on the Monterey Peninsula for thirty years and was the curator of the Del Monte Art Gallery. There is no mention made whether she heard music coming from the wall. The original adobe was moved from Alvarado Street to Mesa Road.

The Rose

A cutting from the Sherman Rose is said to have been transplanted to an Inn, appropriately called the Sherman Rose

Inn. If you are in Monterey drop by both the original site of the old adobe and the inn; you just might run into Senorita Bonifacio smelling her fragrant roses. {10}

Location

The Sherman Adobe is located on Calle Principal next to the Larkin House. The adobe served as General William Sherman's quarters from 1847-1849. The house is not open to the public but the Larkin House is. You must reserve your place in advance for a tour inside the home.

"Who gather round and wonder at the tale Of horrid apparition tall and ghastly, that walks at dead of night."
~ The Grave, Robert Blair

Sawmill Gulch ~ Pebble Beach

Ghostly Snapshot

The Monterey cypress is a striking tree, with its massive limbs growing in twisted patterns. A garden book will tell you the strong ocean winds molded the trees branches into their contorted state but there is a legend that claims a broken heart had more to do with their tortured form than any strong wind.

The Romantic Legend

Through the thick grove of trees a young man rode. This was his last week in Monterey and the errand he was on from the court of Spain had turned into a frustrating endeavor. He was certain he was trapped in the fabled Minotaur labyrinth with each promising lead taking him nowhere. Oh the people of Monterey had been friendly of course and welcomed him into their small community but he was not there to be an extra dance partner at a fandango. The coming voyage home would be hard to bear but displeasing the court was even worse.

For months he had been looking for a thief. This was not a new crime but one that occurred many years previous. The man in question did not rob the court of gold, nor was he an embezzler. His crime was running off with one of the nobles'

Twisted boughs.

daughters. The girl's father was now seriously ill. His dying wish was to see his daughter once more and bring the perpetrator of this crime to justice. It was rumored the thief, Pedro Travasos, had taken the girl to a distant Spanish colony – but which one? Year after year inquiries were made of every returning ship, but it was as if the man's daughter had simply vanished. That is until news reached the father of a town called Monterey with a thriving settlement. The father wondered if perhaps in such a place it would be easy to go undetected. And, as it turned out, he was correct.

For the past seventeen years a miller, his wife, and daughter lived simply in a grove of cypress near Monterey. He was an industrious man in a useful occupation. The town was growing and with the influx of new people, Monterey needed such tradesmen. There was nothing about their life that should draw the suspicion of others.

Down the rough wagon road Don Artega went. There was no real reason for going this way other that he hadn't traveled it before. The miller, his wife, and his daughter warmly received him. A guest to the mill was always welcome as the family rarely traveled into town. Don Artega was instantly drawn to their daughter, Gabriela, who with a warm smile and winning manner made him feel at ease. This chance encounter of course led to weekly visits. The miller and his wife were apprehensive, but not wanting to arouse Don Artega's suspicion, they could only be courteous and to his mission plead ignorance.

After all these years away from Spain they had assumed they had been forgotten – but what to do now? With their lives so well established in Monterey, the idea of fleeing and enduring the same hardships again was not conceivable. And more importantly they had never told Gabriela their secret.

And so it was that Don Artega, seated in their salon after months of courting Gabriela, came to ask for her hand. His original errand pushed to the back of his mind these past happy months had landed back in his lap in the form of a letter from the court demanding his immediate return. The captain of the vessel who delivered the letter himself to the small boarding house where Don Artega had rented rooms was only in port long enough to stock up on provisions for the long voyage back. Don Artega resolved to bring back with him a bride, a "wild rose" as he had taken to call Gabriela.

The couple was married at the Mission San Carlos de Borremeo. The priest noted that the parents seemed reserved in their joy but simply thought they were sad to see their only daughter move so far away. Putting his hand on Don Castro's shoulders he said, "Rejoice, your Gabriela has found a good man. They will return one day, you wait and see." The miller managed a weak smile and thanked the padre.

Days at the mill became longer. The miller and his wife awaited news from Gabriela. Had her voyage gone well? Was she finding life with her in-laws manageable? A full year passed in the gulch before a letter was received. Color slowly drained from the miller's face as his wife read the letter out loud to him. Gabriela it said was to be presented at court.

On the day of the presentation an old minister noticed a striking similarity between Gabriela and the woman who had been abducted years before. Don Artega was taken aside and questioned at length by the minister as to the girl's parentage. Don Artega was shocked. Perhaps his love for Gabriela had blinded him to inconsistencies in the miller's story of how he came to be in Monterey. He realized how very little he had learned in those months spent in the company of the miller and his wife. And as for his bride, who Don Artega truly did love, how could he break the truth to her? Better for him to wait until the man was arrested and had been dealt with. Don Artega told Gabriela that he must travel for the King and would return in a few months.

Unbeknownst to him, Gabriela learned the truth from her maid. Deciding that she could not see her father returned to Spain, she followed her husband. She stowed away and when discovered was given accommodation below deck and kept out of sight. Upon reaching Monterey, Gabriela managed to elude her husband and hastened on horseback, along the dirt road to the dark thicket of cypress she had called home.

The miller and his wife's joy at seeing Gabriela was short-lived when they learned the deputies were but moments away. The old miller, ready with his gun, swore he would never return to Spain nor allow his wife to be taken from him.

As Don Artega strode towards the home, shots rang out. Kicking down the door Don Artega saw sprawled on the floor the miller and his wife, then he noticed a third shadow. He slowly approached, not wanting to see what he already knew. It is said upon hearing his agonized cries the cypress treetops withered. {11}

Manifestations

Do the spirits of Don Artega and Gabriela still wander through the gulch? In the evening hours on especially stormy nights, Don Artega's cries have been heard. The spirits have also been spotted on moonless nights wandering through the trees.

It is not possible to determine with preciseness the origin of this legend. But with its gothic overtones and Romeo and Juliet inspired love story it probably dates to the late 1800s. New settlers to North America might have felt engulfed by nature. This fear manifested itself in ghost tales such as this.

Location

Sawmill Gulch is an abandoned sand quarry in the woods on land owned by the Pebble Beach Company. The area is closed to the existing Country Club and Pacific Grove Gates/Hwy 1 Gates.

"True love is like ghosts, which everybody talks about and few have seen."

~ Francois de la Rochefoucauld

The Lady in Lace ~ Pebble Beach

Ghostly Snapshot

A deserted stretch of road, a misty night, and the image of a woman suddenly appear in your headlights. You swerve; looking in the rear view you see nothing. What was that you ask your passengers? "Oh that," they reply matter of factly. That was just the Lady in Lace, one of the best-known phantoms in the area.

Manifestations

In the 1980s, a couple left their home to visit friends in the neighboring town of Carmel. They had traveled this stretch of highway many times before. Although there was a chill in the air, it was a beautiful night for a romantic, moonlit drive. They reached Pescadero Point in the early evening and took the bend in the road that led to a small parking lot. They had plans to sit on the rocks for a while and take in the magnificent view. This was the best time of night as tour buses and most tourists had returned to their hotels.

Relaxing in the quiet glow of the moonlight, the hours slipped by quickly. The next time the man glanced at his watch it was in the early hours of the morning. They were just about to head home when they heard someone approaching from behind. They turned to see a woman walking towards the shoreline. While it was odd to see a lone woman out this late at night, what was odder was her apparel – a lace wedding dress. She moved slowly as if dragged down by some unseen weight.

The couple watched the woman until she disappeared behind a cypress tree. Thinking she may be in some sort of distress, the man went in search but could find no trace of her.

The phantom lady of 17-Mile Drive has been seen for years. Usually at dusk she is known to walk this road in the vicinity of the Ghost Tree. She gives drivers the scare of their lives, suddenly appearing in their headlights in the center of the road.

The Lady in Lace is a forlorn ghost whose identity is speculated upon. She could be waiting for her seaman fiancé to return from a voyage he never will, a jilted bride or even a well-known historic figure.

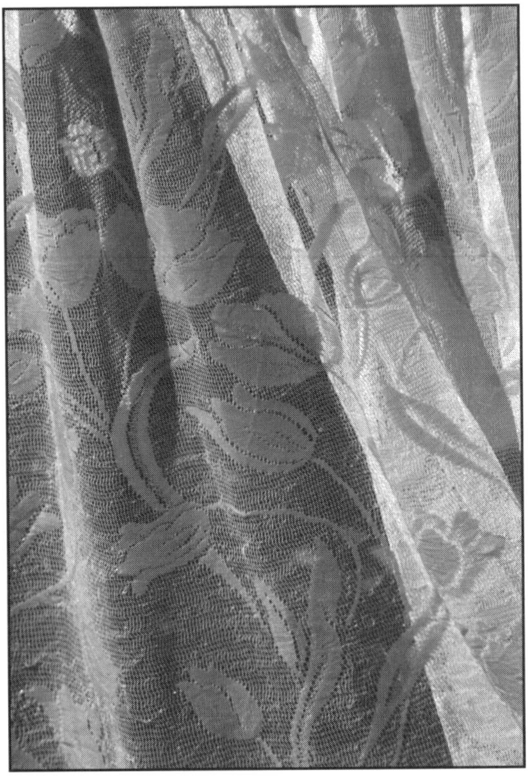

Look for the Lady in Lace, in Pebble Beach, California.

The prevalent theory is the Lady in Lace is none other than the spirit of Dona Maria del Carmen Barreto, who once owned a large piece of land in the Pebble Beach area.

History

In January of 1836, Fabian Berreto petitioned Governor Gutierrez for a grant of land called Pescadero. The land grant extending from Point Lobos to Point Cypress was confirmed in 1840. The next year Fabian Berreto died, leaving Maria in possession of the ranch. She lived there until 1846 and then sold it for a measly $500 or 4,398 acres for a little less than twelve cents an acre. Maria then moved into the town of Monterey. What convinced her to sell this land for such a paltry sum we shall never know. For ghost trackers the question is – is Maria still mourning her lost land?

What Does It Mean?

Could the appearance of a white phantom have a deeper meaning? In the *Oxnard Daily Courier* a curious article appeared in 1921 touting the good and bad qualities of phantoms. If the phantom appears clad in white, your prosperity and happiness will increase. If you are the wife of a sailor, his ship will come safe into port. If the phantom is clad in black, your money will disappear and your life struggles only increase.

Location

The lodge is located at 1700 17-Mile Drive. From Highway 1 turn west on Highway 68, turn south onto 17-Mile Drive and follow the coastal road to the hotel. Phone: (831) 654-9300. There is an interactive map on the Pebble Beach Resorts' website for directions. See www.pebblebeach.com

"Apparitions are often confused with hauntings. The difference is that apparitions are 'live' (intelligent consciousness) and hauntings are 'recordings'."

~ Loyd Auerbach

The Ghost of Monterey ~ Monterey

Ghostly Snapshot

The star-crossed lovers are forced to ride the grey steed into eternity. They may never rest and never truly be happy together. They ride at night when the fog rolls in. He is dressed in a cloak and the girl sitting behind him wears a black gown and lace mantilla.

The Triangle

Don Diego was a gregarious man who liked his drink and the ladies. Had it not been for the fact that Don Diego was a married man, this would not have been a problem. The padre often warned him of his ways. If Don Diego had been a wise man he would have taken note, his wife was growing angrier at each flirtation.

His wife, Manuela, was feared by most people in the town. It was rumored she had bewitched Don Diego into marrying her. How else could such an odd couple come together? The mission Indians did not trust Manuela and believed her capable of witchcraft. There was talk Manuela even practiced magic in the hillsides and cavorted with ghosts.

One day a large fandango was held at the home of a good friend; as usual Manuela refused to go. Don Diego went alone. He feasted and danced and ended up spending much of the night with one woman. At the end of the evening Don Diego and his new love decided to leave together.

Don Diego, without a care in the world, mounted his horse and helped the woman on behind. From out of the shadows Don Diego's wife suddenly appeared. She placed a curse on the couple that they would never rest and in death their ghosts would still ride.

Manifestations

Don Diego and Manuela were never seen in the flesh again. Some say the wife killed the pair on the spot. Others say she was a witch who convinced her followers to kill the couple. When the fog rolls in you can still see the doomed couple riding their ghostly horse in the countryside around Monterey.

"Thou distant tree, whose lonely top Has bent to many a storm, No more canst thou deceive my hope, and take my lover's form"

~ Joanna Baillie

4

The Bandits

The Hail of Stones

Ghostly Snapshot

If this story is true, justice may catch up with criminals but death doesn't slow them down.

The Bungalow

With its large porch supported by thick, square columns and double hung windows, the small bungalow was one of the nicest on the block. Now with windowpanes destroyed and shards of glass littering the lawn, people hurry by fearing that they too will bring the demon back to their homes. Some even avoid the street completely. Others ask for exorcism. At local stores some think it should be burned down. But his home isn't abandoned nor is it the headquarters of a criminal but a dead bandit might have something to do with why it is in its present state.

This story begins not in San Jose but in Monterey, the birthplace of Tiburcio Vasquez. You can still stroll down Dutra Street today and see his family's adobe, now the property of the City of Monterey, a few hundred yards from the old jail. The location seems fitting as this man embarked on a notorious criminal career. The current pink two-story adobe is quite altered from the one room adobe Tiburcio Vasquez would have been familiar with, thanks to many renovations undertaken by Louis Hill, one of California's railroad tycoons.

The Vasquez Adobe, Monterey, California. Guadalupe Cantua de Vasquez purchased the home in the 1830s.

Tiburcio Vasquez was a charming bandit who could hold you up at the stage coach stop and the next minute be buying you a drink at the local tavern and commiserating over your misfortune. A celebrity of sorts who when he was captured, after eluding the law for many years, hundreds of ladies came to the jail in San Jose to see him. The courtroom was packed daily with his admirers. It is no wonder that he is thought to be the model for the fictional character Zorro. But all the admirers in the world could not save Tiburcio from the hangman's noose. On March 19, 1875, he was hung in the county jail, San Jose, Santa Clara County, for the murder of Lander Davidson at Tres Pinos.

The following story takes place sixty miles north in the city of San Jose. This is the story of Tiburcio Vasquez and a man called Mr. Reardon. Mr. Reardon was an architect – quite a good architect from all accounts. He had no enemies, was a respectable man, and a good employee. A reporter would later note that Mr. Reardon's designs had not affronted the good people of San Jose nor what happened to Mr. Reardon "...*[sic]* a reflection of the American peoples' attitude towards architects in general."

In May 1876, almost a year after Tiburcio's hanging, Mr. Reardon was in his home when he heard a loud thump. Angrily,

Mr. Reardon raced to the door. "Those blasted children would think twice about throwing stones at his home," he thought. A blast of cold air greeted him as he looked out onto a deserted street; at his feet he saw a couple of large rocks.

During the next few evenings, the same thing occurred. Mr. Reardon wasted no time in contacting the local authorities but they weren't concerned with a neighborhood prankster. By the fourth night though, it was clear that this was more than a case of local boys. First a window was taken out, then another. The rocks weren't just being hurled one by one anymore; they were more akin to a hailstorm.

Neighbors noted that from nowhere rocks would fall on Mr. Reardon's home. Not just pebbles but large, fist-sized rocks being hurled by unseen hands. Oddly, no other homes were affected.

At last Mr. Reardon was forced to abandon his house and take up residence in another house built by a rival architect. Mr. Reardon felt relieved to be in his new home but his relief would soon turn to dread. In the early evening hours as he sat down for his evening meal, there was a thump, followed by another thump. "Someone was playing a nasty trick on him," thought Mr. Reardon. His eyes shifted nervously from side to side. Incredulously, the very first evening in his new home was heralded by what the papers would later call "a perfect tornado of stones."

In the morning the police came but the stone shower showed no signs of slackening. What had Mr. Reardon done to bring this upon himself? One time is odd but two times would surely indicate something more sinister at play – something otherworldly perhaps?

The weather bureau could offer no reasonable explanation. The only odd weather occurrences, such as toads falling from the sky, had been reported in France more than one hundred years ago. The bureau maintained there was nothing out of the order in the weather, certainly nothing to explain this biblical-like occurrence.

His new yard was soon covered in stones sixteen to eighteen inches deep. These very same stones were seen by one awe-stricken policeman, "to lift themselves up and hurl themselves, without the aid of any visible hand, through the wrecked window sashes." As a last resort, a distraught Mr. Reardon called in a spiritual medium. He promised to pay any medium the sum of $5 if they could explain this bizarre occurrence and the exorbitant sum of $10 if they could materialize the stone thrower.

One medium, whose name did not appear in print, answered Mr. Reardon's appeal. A crowd gathered at the house, perhaps hoping the phantom would appear and watched the medium as he surveyed the damage. After some considerable time the medium announced before the assembled media that the stone thrower was none other than Tiburcio Vasquez returned from the dead.

Mr. Reardon was stunned by this news. Why would Tiburcio Vasquez target him? He had never met the man in his entire life. A *New York Times* reporter, in which this story appeared, dug a little more and discovered the curse of Tiburcio. According to the *New York Times*, Tiburcio Vasquez promised before he was hung to "...return from ghostland and surprise those of his fellow-citizens who had failed to protest against his hanging." In May 1876 he did this very thing by coming back from the grave.

As proof of Tiburcio Vasquez's return, the medium claimed the rocks littering Mr. Reardon's lawn were not local to San Jose. No, these special stones were in fact identical with the stones abundant in the distant mountains where Mr. Vasquez hid from the law.

Sadly, the medium failed to materialize Mr. Vasquez. With $5 in pocket nothing more was heard of him.

As for Mr. Reardon, his predicament was so widely publicized he was not able to rent another home. The local Chinese community held nightly picnics in front of his house to witness the spectacle. Who would dare rent to a man so cursed?

Mr. Reardon then fades from San Jose history. It was reported that he was considering a move far from San Jose – to a distant region where Mr. Vasquez could not come. {12, 13}

Manifestations

If you are walking along Dutra Street in Monterey and you feel a cold breeze sweep towards you, followed by a hard tap on your shoulder, don't be surprised if it is a rock. Flickering lights and footsteps have occurred inside the Vasquez Adobe. One worker who did not wish to be identified reported a strange feeling of someone or something near his desk although he was alone at the time. He called it a night before anything stranger occurred. The presence at the home has never been identified but from the previous story of Mr. Reardon if it is Tiburcio he has returned a much calmer spirit! If you do not want this spirit at your house, offering up a prayer to the deceased Tiburcio Vasquez might be a good idea, though he is supposed to be resting in the Catholic Cemetery of Santa Clara, California.

Location

The Vasquez adobe is located at 546 Dutra Street in Monterey. It is conveniently located behind the jail and Colton Hall. The home is not open to the public as it houses offices for The City of Monterey.

"...either his aunt or himself was unwittingly a physical medium, it meant that they were simply aiding to focus the forces of a haunted house already charged to the brim. It was like walking with unprotected lamps among uncovered stores of gunpowder."

~ The Empty House, Algernon Blackwood

The Headless Spirit of Joaquin Murrieta ~ Monterey

"If before breakfast you happen to see a black cat, three lame fellows on one and the same street or a corpse, it would be better for you to go back home and stay indoors for the day, because something wrong is in store for you."

~ Mexican superstition, author unknown, June 23, 1907

Ghostly Snapshot

This headless ghost has terrified people for over one hundred years. Does the spirit of Joaquin Murrieta ride nightly in the direction of the Carmel Mission?

The Life of a Bandit

Joaquin Murrieta was, by all accounts, a pleasant young man who gave no outward sign or at least none that were detected of the infamous exploits he would later be associated with. Author John Rollin Ridges's writes in his *Yellow Bird, Life &*

Relief carving of the Carmel Mission. Location – Junipero Serra Monument, Vizcaino Landing Site.

Adventures of Joaquin Murieta: The Celebrated California Bandit (1955 University of Oklahoma Press), "(he) gave no sign of the indomitable and daring spirit which afterwards characterized him." Joaquin Murrieta before the age of twenty would rack up so many "daring" acts he became one of the most notorious bandits in Los Angeles County, Monterey County, and up to San Jose. Countless sorties were credited to him but they could have been the work of other men. There were other Joaquins operating in the same area.

The Carmel Mission

It was here at the Carmel Mission a padre gave shelter to Joaquin Murieta, hiding from rangers after running into trouble in the Santa Clara Valley. During his stay at the mission, Joaquin is said to have found a tunnel leading to the padres' lost silver mine! In another related story he stashes his own treasure in the padre's tunnel. The restless spirit of Joaquin is sighted frequently in the area.

The Haunting of Billy Henderson

Billy Henderson was a doomed man. It hadn't always been this way. He had a nice spread and his ranch was doing all right. His mistake had been riding with Captain Harry Love in pursuit of Joaquin Murieta. Upon finding Joaquin Murieta's hideout, it had taken one bullet to bring this outlaw down. What happened next haunted Billy Henderson for the rest of his life.

Not satisfied with merely killing Joaquin Murieta or his deputy, three fingered Jack, the men decided to decapitate Joaquin and chop off the hand of three-fingered Jack. With such proof they hoped to claim their reward in Sacramento.

From that day on, Billy Henderson told his friends he was haunted by the spirit of Joaquin, "...*[sic]* there was not a day, or more usually a night, that Joaquin did not come to him (Billy) personally, headless, and speak—for his voice was recognizable even though his head was missing. He was always demanding his head."

The first time Billy saw the apparition he was riding from Los Angeles to his ranch. It was daylight when a horseman appeared out of nowhere. "I am Joaquin Murrieta," replied the strange horseman, in a voice so uncanny and yet so natural that its effect was absolutely startling. "You cut my head off, and I want you to restore it to me. No rest will ever come to me until I get my head back." (*On The Old West Coast* by Major Horace Bell. William Morrow & Co., NY 1930)

The Head

Joaquin Murieta's head and the hand of three fingered Jack were preserved in alcohol. The jars were exhibited at Natchez's Arms Store & Pistol Gallery on Clay Street in San Francisco. In the book, *Searching for Joaquin: Myth, Murieta, and History in California* (Encounter Books 2003), Bruce Thornton writes, the auction of Joaquin's head generated its own legend. "When Sheriff Harrison dropped the gavel on the sale, an Irishman cried out, "Oh! Is it possible that you are going to sell the head of your fellow-creature!" and predicted bad luck for both seller and buyer." p.149.

The Curse

A rumor attached to the jar containing Joaquin's head cursed those involved in his capture. Proof of this was the bad end that came to those involved in the capture. The Sheriff committed suicide; Natchez accidentally killed himself while examining a pistol; Byrnes went insane; and spirits for the rest of his life plagued Henderson. Mr. Craigmiles, who according to *The San Joaquin Republican* of February 1856 was the next owner of the head, planned on exhibiting the head on a tour of the Atlantic States. Maybe curse rumors got to him as he soon sold it. In 1865 the head was part of Dr. Jordan's Pacific Museum of Anatomy and Science on Market Street, San Francisco. When an earthquake destroyed the museum in 1906, Joaquin's severed head was blamed! {14, 15}

Location

The gunfight between Harry Love's rangers and the Murrieta gang is near the intersection of Interstate 5 and Highway 33.

Manifestations

There are reports in the Carmel Valley and along the Pacheco Pass of drivers swerving to avoid horsemen materializing out of the fog. In the years after his death Joaquin Murieta was seen searching for his head or swimming in the Taloumne (Tuolumne) River carrying his head. Other non-ghostly tales tell of him living out his days in Mexico.

"...modern thought is much divided on spiritual phenomena. For every 'well-attested' ghost investigated and pronounced genuine, there is equally plausible 'explanation' usually supplied by some one whose authority is undoubted."

~ W.B. Northrop writing in 1907.

Anastasio Garcia ~ Monterey

Ghostly Snapshot

The old Monterey Jail is now part of a historic walking tour but with stories of prisoners hung from their cells and wagons used to lead others away are still heard.

The Old Monterey Jail, Monterey, California. The building was constructed in 1854. It only has six prisoner cells.

History

"Native prisoners, arrested for robbery and confined in the adobe jail at Monterey, clamored for their guitars, and the nights were filled with music until the rascals swung at half mast."

~ Charles Warren Stoddard

Perhaps moans rather than music filled the air around the old jail. The site of more than one lynching and a jailhouse hanging, it is no wonder that the Monterey jail has its fair share of paranormal happenings. It was here in 1857 one of California's outlaws met his death, not at the hands of the law, but rather at the hands of the "good" citizens of Monterey. The following story from a February 1857 issue of the *Daily Alta*, "Late News from Monterey" tells "... a party of men broke into the jail at that place, ... And hung the notorious outlaw Anastacio Garcia who was confined therein awaiting trial for murder." Garcia, a native of California, was described in the 1857 article as being handsome – "The very beau ideal of a brigand—physical excellence, reckless courage skilled in the use of arms, an air little short of romance." When he was hung he was only twenty-eight years of age.

Anastacio Garcia

Anastacio Garcia's first documented crime was the killing of young constable Hardmount at a fandango. He was never brought to trial for this crime as he hid out until most of the witnesses disappeared. The slayings of Isaac Wall and Thomas Williamson would lead to his incarceration. Anastacio Garcia was captured when his wife was followed to his hideout.

On February 17, 1857, a visitor entering the Monterey jail found the sheriff and deputy tied up. Upon being freed they went to Garcia's cell and found his body hanging from the rafters.

Manifestations

Reports from the Old Jail include unusual sounds, music, and voices when the jail is closed. The sensation of being touched on the back of the neck and an overwhelming sense of fear, which could be explained by the setting. The jail is a tight, cramped place with several cells set up to resemble the way they looked when the jail was operational.

In the cell where Anastasio Garcia was hung, psychics have detected a presence indicating the violent acts that occurred in this space have left an invisible scar. One psychic suggested the spirit could be a man named Otis Hall. Otis Hall has the unfortunate claim to fame for being "...the first victim of a lynch mob in the central coast region." He was killed in the jail for taking part in the 1851 murder of John Caldwell, a mail rider between Monterey and Los Angeles. {16}

Location

Located next to Colton Hall. The Old Jail was built in 1854 and used as the City Jail until 1956. Pacific Street (between Jefferson and Madison Streets) Phone: (831) 646-5628. It is open to the public. The cells are set up to recreate a few famous visitors and fictional ones.

"...[sic] he who shall look through the knot-hole in the plank of the coffin shall acquire the evil eye."

~ The Black Reaper, Bernard Capes

The Wagon Wheels ~ Monterey

With at least three haunted structures, is it any wonder that the street itself is home to a few phantoms as well?

Manifestations

Two visitors to Monterey were walking on Dutra Street as they had visited Colton Hall. The street was deserted as it was just starting to rain. To the man's annoyance he had left his umbrella at the hall, so he raced back before it was locked up for the night. The lady waited for him just in front of the Vasquez adobe. She absently flipped through a brochure until a rumbling and squeaking sound caught her attention. Without looking up, she stepped further back to the side of the road. Squeeeeak. This time she looked up and saw nothing. Puzzled she looked up and down the street.

Then she could heard the neighing of horses. Scared out of her wits, the woman took off in her husband's direction, who by this time was returning umbrella in hand. She told him what had happened. Did this woman hear the road as it once was with the pounding of horse hooves? Perhaps the wagon the horse was pulling was the one used to transport one infamous prisoner to his death. We shall never know but the following is the true story of a man called Tarpy and his final wagon ride from the jail.

Matt Tarpy

On March 17, 1873, an Irish immigrant farmer landowner and political activist named Matt Tarpy was accused of killing a woman—Mrs. Sarah Nicholson—in cold blood. He was dragged from his jail cell by an angry mob and hanged from a tree in the outskirts of Monterey. The ill-fated plot of land became known as Tarpy's Flats and the story remained legend even after Charles A Ryan bought the nearby 454 acres of rolling hills & meadows in 1917 and built a roadside house for his family. Today, the stone house is said to be haunted by Matt Tarpy. It is now one of the Peninsula's most celebrated restaurants – Tarpy's Roadhouse.

Matt Tarpy had been well liked. He was someone who defended the property of neighbors. Born in Ireland, he immigrated to California by way of San Francisco in 1851. He was involved in politics and lived in Santa Cruz with his wife and three daughters.

A display wagon.

He was the driving force behind a vigilante group – Pajaro Property Protective Society – they were formed to combat gangs of horse thieves and cattle rustlers.

Tarpy had his share of enemies. He was a strong advocate of the lynch law. As such, he never went anywhere unarmed. To his friends, however, he was kind and generous.

What led to his eventual death was the selling of four hundred acres of his 1500 acres to Murdock and Sara Nicholson in 1868. Mr. Nicholson was a carriage maker. The boundaries were never clearly defined and a dispute broke out over a piece of land along the San Juan Road. While Murdock was called away on business, Tarpy moved a cabin onto the property and rented it to a German named Peterson. When she learned of this, Mrs. Nicholson rode into town and consulted a lawyer, J. A. Barham. He advised that she still held the deed and that she could not be put out of her property without due legal process. She moved a few things into the home and the boy who helped on the farm and another man O'Neill took possession of it. In the middle of the night, Matt Tarpy fired shots into the home and when the occupants ran out he fired again, killing Sara. He was taken to Monterey because of its secure jail. It would turn out to not be secure enough.

On Saturday the whole population of Watsonville turned out to express sympathy for the victim and denounce the murder. At her funeral a speech was made "if you allow this murderer to go unchanged twenty-four hours longer you are all cowards..." Crowds started to gather in Monterey demanding that Matt Tarpy be taken to Salinas—the sheriff left for the telegraph office and read the Judge's orders that the prisoner was to be kept in Monterey—the crowd took this opportunity to seize the sheriff and bind him up. They then sent a dispatch to Salinas, "To the Public of Salinas City: Watson bound hand and foot." March 17, 1873.

Begging for his life, the mob dragged Matt Tarpy from his cell and drove three miles out of town to a pine tree. He was allowed to draw up a brief will and he addressed the crowd for thirty minutes. When he was finally hung, his neck did not break. He died an agonizing death by strangulation. {17}

Manifestations

The sound of wheels, voices, and even horses neighing have been reported by the jail. Is Matt Tarpy's last journey being replayed again and again?

Location

The restaurant Tarpy's Roadhouse is located on Highway 68 and Canyon Del Rey, Monterey. 29999 Monterey Salinas Hwy. The house dates back to the 1880s. The website www.tarpys.com has detailed directions. Phone: (831) 647-1444

"The lawn is pressed by unseen feet, and ghosts return gently at twilight, gently go at dawn.."

~ T.S. Eliot, To Walter de la Mare

5

Haunted Landmarks

Robert Louis Stevenson House ~ Monterey

Ghostly Snapshot

The lady in the black dress has been seen everywhere in this building by staff and visitors. What is it about an upstairs bedroom that she can't leave behind? The Robert Louis Stevenson House in Monterey, formerly The French Hotel, is known as one of the most haunted homes in Monterey.

Robert Louis Stevenson house.

History

Robert Louis Stevenson plaque.

With ghostly sightings, rattling latches, the odor of disinfectant (carbolic acid), and objects moving by unseen hands, the Robert Louis Stevenson house has all the elements of a good gothic novel. But this is no fictionalized setting; it is a home on Monterey's Path of History walking tour now known as the Robert Louis Stevenson house. Edith Van Antwerp and C. Tobin Clark rescued the home, which once faced demolition. They raised money to completely restore the adobe, which Robert Louis Stevenson (1850-1893) called home during his four-month stay in Monterey.

Why did Robert Louis Stevenson travel all the way from Scotland to this remote place? Why, for love, of course. Robert Louis Stevenson had fallen madly in love with Frances (Fanny) Osbourne while she was staying in Grez, France, with her daughter, Bella. Upon returning to the States, she would send a telegram to the author informing him that she had filed for divorce. Not content to wait in Europe until Fanny's divorce was finalized, Robert Louis Stevenson traveled by ship to the States. Having suffered from bronchial infections since childhood, the sea voyage took its toll. Robert Louis Stevenson documents his voyage in his book *The Amateur Emigrant*. Shortly after his arrival in Monterey, Robert Louis Stevenson became very ill, but made a full recovery thanks to new friends like Jules Simoneau, who kept a restaurant in the French Hotel. Robert Louis Stevenson married Fanny, May 19, 1880, living one year in the States before first returning to Europe and later Samoa, where the writer would die suddenly from a cerebral hemorrhage. While Fanny did consult spiritual mediums in an attempt to contact Stevenson after his death, these were never held in Monterey but in her San Francisco dwelling on Hyde Street. It is interesting to note Fanny left her San Francisco home in 1906 after becoming convinced it was haunted by evil entities.

As tempting as it is for Stevenson aficionados to believe the famous author, who found inspiration in Monterey to write his classics *Treasure Island* and *This Old Pacific Capital*, haunts the home, it is believed the ghost of Manuela Girardin actually still resides at 530 Houston Street. The two-story adobe built around 1830 by Don Rafael Gonzalez was later sold to Girardin, a Swiss businessman who expanded the original two-story adobe, thus creating a rooming house. It was in this rooming house, for a time known as The French Hotel, that Robert Louis Stevenson stayed. A former curator of the Stevenson House, Barbara Burdick, told author Antoinette May of her encounter with Mrs. Girardin for the book *Haunted Houses of California*. "She was oddly dressed in a long gown with a high lace collar, but aside from that looked as 'lively' as anyone. Despite the stories, it never occurred to me that she wasn't just another tourist. When I explained that it was closing time, she nodded understandingly. I turned to leave and then looked back, wondering just how she had managed to get inside the barred room. The nursery was empty."

Manifestations

Sightings of Mrs. Girardin are not limited to guides, but also include visitors. She is sometimes glimpsed out of the corner of an eye. One visiting teacher thought she saw a white flash darting into a room. Thinking it was one of her more challenging pupils, she went looking but no one was there and the child in question was accounted for. More often Mrs. Girardin is a moving figure on the narrow staircase. A rocking chair is also known to move back and forth until an image of a woman dressed in black appears. Just as quickly as she arrived, she vanishes, leaving behind bewildered guests.

One of the most unnerving accounts of Mrs. Girardin comes from an elementary schoolchild. The child on a school trip to the home was able to see the home as it was during the late 1800s. No, he wasn't giving a description of period furnishings or reading from a California Parks and Recreation pamphlet, but was seeing people no one else could see. As the school group moved from room to room, the boy vividly described to his teacher what had happened in the home. Looking into the nursery, he saw two children ill in bed with a woman dressed in black tending to them. In another room on the upper level, he saw a man lying in a bed coughing, his chest heaving up and down.

The guide was very impressed and wondered how the child had come to learn so much about the house. This was definitely not a daily occurrence with any group, especially not with a school group where running through the garden was generally the highlight. This boy certainly saw more than anyone else that day. The teacher listening to his running commentary was intrigued, if not amused, but hadn't for a moment thought he was correct until the guide affirmed that indeed two children had been very ill in the home.

Those children were Manuela Girardin's grandchildren, who she cared for night and day when they took ill with typhoid. She sadly succumbed to the disease herself, but the children recovered. It is said that many unexplainable occurrences happen in December, the month Mrs. Girardin died. It would seem that even in death Mrs. Girardin is looking after her grandchildren.

Location

The French Hotel now known as the Stevenson House is located at 530 Houston Street.

The home is open to visitors but like other structure on Monterey's historic walking path, visitors must register for tours in advance.

Telephone : 831-649-7118.

The home is part of a historic walking tour of Monterey. It is a whitewashed building with the words French Hotel still visible.

"A new world, material without being real, poor ghosts, breathing dreams like air, drifted fortuitously about...like that ashen fantastic figure gliding toward through the amorphous tress."

~ F. Scott Fitzgerald, The Great Gatsby

First Theatre ~ Monterey

Ghostly Snapshot

A ghost called Jack has been scaring people in a theatre for close to a hundred years now. Who was he and what does he want?

Excerpt from a Poem on Theatre Door

"Many a miner passed though this door
who swore he would never come in any more.
Twas here they eased him of nuggets of gold."

History

So reads a wooden sign above the modest door to this adobe. And many a miner did pass through this door on his way to, and back from, the gold rush. One of these miners was Jack Swan. But to call him a miner is perhaps a bit misleading. Jack Swan held many positions in

The First Theatre, Monterey, California. Located on the southwest corner of Pacific and Scot Streets.

The First Theatre garden, Monterey, California.

his lifetime. He first arrived in Monterey in 1843 from England and built the "First Theatre" as it had come to be known in 1844. The structure itself was built by Jack Swan from lumber salvaged from a shipwreck. He added on the lodging house in 1846.

Manifestations

The question today for the group of tourists listening to a well rehearsed talk on the history of the theatre is whether or not someone is still inside? For more than a two hundred years, plays have been staged at this small, unassuming adobe. Rumors of footsteps in the area used to keep the props and other unusual noises would seem to indicate a presence, but whose? According to locals, Jack Swan himself haunts the theatre. But why would he return to this building, as history states that he spent many years away from Monterey?

Jack Swan

Alfred (Jack) Swan was a sailor of Scottish descent who came to Monterey as a crew member on the Soledad, a

Mexican brig engaged in the coastal trade between Mexico and Alta, California. Upon arriving, he decided to stay and soon was hired on by John B.R. Cooper, a man of much historical importance in Monterey. He was hired as ship's cook but at the end of 1844 he was back in Monterey. Whether he was fired or jumped ship is unknown. Around this time he decided to set himself up as a pie maker. Yes, a pie maker. Perhaps not the sort of work you'd expect from an ex-sailor but then again maybe his cooking skills were the best. His business must have enjoyed some success, as he was able to buy a piece of land.

The "First Theatre" as it is called today was used as a boarding house for sailors, a saloon, used for storing whaling equipment, and – as the name indicates – a theatre. Was Jack missing some of the life he was used to in England? This question is never answered. Though he wrote extensively about his experiences in California, little mention is ever made of the years before he came.

In 1847, four army volunteers and three local characters joined forces for two minstrel performances in the unused dining room. A few members of Col. Jonathan D. Stevenson's regiment gave an outdoor performance and, encouraged by their success, persuaded Jack Swan to remodel the building for dramatic performances.

By 1849 Gold Rush fever was sweeping through California and many from Monterey left for the mines; among them was one Jack Swan. Jack Swan leased his building to a number of businesses: whaling station, drug dispensary, tearoom, and shop. He traveled in and out of Monterey over the next thirty-five years. From the late 1860s to the 1890s, Uncle John Swan, as he came to be known, lived a life bordering on poverty. The hunt for gold would lead him to Victoria, British Columbia. He wrote frequently for papers such as the *Monterey Bulletin*, *The Santa Cruz Sentinel,* and *The San Jose Pioneer*. When at home he lived in Monterey, but much of his time was spent in San Antonio, still searching for the fortune in gold that eluded him. He lost his remaining property and spent his final years as a county charge. On the evening Jan 6, 1896, while walking down a hall in the Monterey County Hospital, he died of a heart attack.

In 1906 a local group of Monterey citizens assisted with funds from W.R. Hearst's California Historic Landmarks League, purchased the building, and deeded it to the state. In 1937 it was leased to Denny-Watrous Management, a performing arts organization dedicated to reviving the performance of melodrama in the old First Theatre. {18, 19}

Still Haunted?

Since the theatre has been closed for over five years for seismic studies and repairs, there have been no new reports of Jack Swan. Has Jack Swan finally passed to the other side now that his beloved theatre is closed or is he waiting in the wings for the next performance? Until the theatre is reopened, we will have to be content with peering through windows and wandering in the backyard. But wouldn't it be wonderful to see "The Troupers of the Gold Coast" perform once more? Perhaps there will be one more in attendance than ticket sales can account for.

Manifestations

One report surfaced many years back about a strange old man dressed in old fashioned clothing crossing the street by the theatre. If this report is correct, the ghost of Jack Swan has taken to wandering the streets of Monterey.

Location

The First Theatre is located at Scott and Pacific Streets. The building is closed to tourists due to seismic investigations. A giant limb of a Sequoia tree in the backyard fell on the building a few years back. There is still a great aura to be felt while walking around the building and peering into windows. This building is also on the historic Monterey walk.

"All the maids got goose flesh and the men fearful to roam about much o'dank, dark nights. For the uneasy spirit kept up its tenancy and its moaning in the corridors and its peeping into the moats."

~ Author unknown, 1906

Merritt House ~ Monterey

Ghostly Snapshot

A beautiful, stately home now operates as an Inn. One of the previous occupants must think it is lovely, as even in death she is said to still reside there.

The Guests

Checking in for a weekend at the historic Merritt House Inn, Dave and Joanne (psued.) had planned on a quiet weekend getaway. They had stayed at the inn before and always found it to be a beautiful place. All began well with a good meal in town, followed by a walk along the water and a leisurely stroll back to their room. The couple's suite was large, complete with their own balcony. A set of steps led down from the balcony to the rooms below. From the balcony, a path lined with roses and an ornate black wrought gate was visible.

The Merritt House, Monterey, California. The home was built in the 1860s. It is named for the first American Judge of Monterey County, Judge Josiah Merritt.

The couple fell asleep quickly, but soon Joanne awoke to a noise outside their door. She listened and heard the sound of footsteps on the stairs. As theirs was the only room on the floor, she was concerned. She walked over to the window. From here she had a clear view of both the staircase and verandah. Peering through the curtain she saw nothing but she could hear the distinct sound of footsteps outside. At one point she thought the footsteps were right outside the window where she was. Her investigation was cut short by the arrival back home of the guests in the suite below.

The Merritt House gate, Monterey, California.

Manifestations

Mysterious footsteps, odd banging, and even the sound of voices when no one is around are just some of the paranormal happenings at the Merritt House.

Location

The Merritt House Inn is located at 386 Pacific Inn, Monterey. (831) 646 9686.

The Inn is listed on the National Register of Historic Places.

The Merritt House was built in 1830. Judge Josiah Merritt and his wife, Juana Castro, raised their five children here. The home was converted into an inn in 1979.

Dr. Elliot Coues, famous ornithologist and member of the Nat'l Academy of Sciences, advocates for belief in the existence of ghosts. "It is obvious, if ghosts exist at all, that they must be made of something. My belief is that they are in a sense substantial and possess a semi-material structure. If you ask what I mean by "semi-material" I will refer for illustration to the ether which is understood to occupy all space."

~ Writing in April 1900

Mission San Carlos Borromeo ~ Carmel

Ghostly Snapshot

Mass unmarked graves, rains revealing skulls, at least two phantoms wandering the gardens, a ghostly rider, and an annual pilgrimage of the dead are but a few of the tales from the Mission San Carlos Borromeo.

History

The Mission founded on June 3, 1770, by Father Junipero Serra was named for Saint Charles Borromeo. It was the second mission in California. The San Carlos Mission was never fully abandoned, but by 1860, when Rev. Angelo D. Casanova was appointed to Monterey, the building was practically destroyed. Without a roof, the inside of the chapel was in ruins and, to make matters worse, souvenir hunters had helped themselves. It would take the dedication of many people to restore it.

Harry Downie devoted fifty years of his life to overseeing the restoration. He began his work on the mission in 1931 when he was appointed curator in charge. For modern day visitors, the grounds of the mission are a place for quiet meditation, to wander through, reading historical markers or to simply admire the basilica. But back when the mission was in a state of neglect, stories of spirits at the mission circulated. The following stories are based on first person accounts, newspaper stories, and even poetry dedicated to the spirits of the mission.

Headless Rider

With a similarity to the *Headless Horseman of Sleepy Hollow* by Irving Washington (1783-1859), this spirit haunts the entire region as far away as Morro Bay. Some believe the phantom rider to be Joaquin Murieta and others think he is a nameless Spanish soldier from one of the expedition parties. Those believing the

Mission San Carlos Borromeo, Carmel, California.

apparition to be Joaquin Murieta point out that frequently the rider is headless. Whoever it is, he haunts the vicinity of the church and the churchyard, and also is seen racing away down the road. Only the rider knows what his nightly quest may be.

"If a ghost is seen hovering about a grave, it is probably the etheric body or shell of a newly buried person. This etheric matter is of a cloudlike formation; though it may be the astral body of a living man haunting in sleep the tomb of a friend..."

A.H.T 1900

Carmel Mission Courtyard ~ Carmel
Ghosts of The Courtyard

Ghostly Snapshot

Are you ever truly alone in the mission's courtyard? Spectral neophytes and mission monks still wander the grounds.

Daily Alta

In an article from January 10, 1858, *Daily Alta California,* "The Mission of Carmel and One of Its Legends" the author writes, *"... [sic] Here and there a skull, uncovered by copious rains appears above ground, as if its owner was desirous to examine into the cause of so great a change. The soul of an aged Indian solitary admits the ruins must mourn the days that will never return, driven from his land – he encounters the graveyard of the church and some bones bleaching upon the grass."*

Manifestations

It was nearly dusk when the visitor to the Mission put away his camera and folded up his brochure. As he stood quietly in the courtyard between the basilica and the school the figure of a small boy caught his eye. Puzzled as to why a child should be by himself in the courtyard the man looked in the direction of the child. In a split second the child disappeared.

The spectral Indian boy is but one of many spirits said to haunt the Carmel Mission. There is also a priest, a

Mission San Carlos Borromeo, Carmel, California.

dog, a horseman, and many more due in no small part to the mission's cemetery containing nearly four thousand unmarked graves. A very famous ghost who is also said to walk through the courtyard and into the church is that of Father Junipero Serra, who passed away here in August 28, 1784. He is said to return to the Mission yearly on the eve of the Feast of San Carlos.

**Note—Mission San Carlos Borromeo de Carmelo is also known as the Carmel Mission

The Feast of San Carlos ~ Carmel

Ghostly Snapshot

Father Serra returns on the feast of San Carlos to say mass. Stories and poems about his return were published from the late 1800s. He doesn't say mass to an empty congregation but one filled with neophytes from Mission Carmel and the surrounding missions. Before you dismiss this as fiction, encounters with fog-like spirits around this date continue to the present day.

The ghost of Father Serra is so devoted to his mission that each year he rises just to say mass. The deceased neophytes not only come from the Carmel mission area but from San Juan Capistrano, Mission San Diego, St. Francis, and San Jose. You will know this ghostly procession is close by if you hear hymns and see censers swinging but no one carrying them. At the first sign of sunrise the phantom congregation simply slips away into the ruins, the weeds, and the very soil of the Carmel Mission. There just might be something to the accounts in the poem written below.

Mission San Carlos Borromeo, Carmel, California.

The Poem

Father Serra's midnight mass from the beyond was immortalized in the poem, "The Midnight Mass," published in 1882 by Richard Coward of San Francisco.

"Tales are told and songs are sung
Of Junipero the Padre
In the sweet Castilian tongue:
Telling how each year he rises
From his grave the mass to say,
In the midnight, mid the ruins,
On the eve of Carlos' day.
THE MIDNIGHT MASS."

More Manifestations

Many have reported seeing a monk and ghostly fog apparitions around the Feast of San Carlos. In the mission's vicinity one woman became panic stricken when she felt presences pressing in on her from all sides, as if she had been caught up in a ghostly march. Did they really mean her any harm? According to the poem the dead do rise around this time on their journey down to the mission.

The Dare ~ Carmel

Ghostly Snapshot

Vandalism is never a wise decision but vandalizing a religious structure is just asking for the devil himself to pay you a personal visit.

The Legend

One young man was dared by his friends to drive a nail into the mission wall. The man, not wanting to appear scared in front of his friends, reluctantly set out for the mission. After an hour had gone by the friends assumed he had changed his mind. They decided to pay him a visit at his home but were informed by the young man's mother that he wasn't there, so they went to the mission in search of him. They found their friend but he was in no condition to go home with them. His face was horribly contorted and his eyes wide with fear, hanging from the very nail they had dared him to drive into the Mission wall.

Mission San Carlos Borromeo, Carmel, California.

Manifestations

The spirit of this man is said to only appear to people contemplating evil acts. Rumors of spirits and of the devil himself walking El Camino Real caused travelers to carve a cross into a tree on the road to ensure safe passage.

"The dark was dying silverly, that strange, still hour when Earth is falling toward the day – That hour of spacious silence and delay when all things poise upon the hinge of change."
~ written by Edwin Markham, 1903

The Cross ~ Monterey

Ghostly Snapshot

In the days after Father Serra said mass at the cross of Monterey and left the area for San Diego, the cross is said to have glowed as if crossed by the hand of God.

History

The expedition returned the following year and was puzzled to find shells, beads, and even fish around the cross. When the Indians were questioned they told a wondrous story of how the cross one evening glowed as if on fire. Not confined to the 1770s, miracles about the cross and later the area where the first mass was held appeared in *The Daily Alta*.

Once, a sick man who knelt at the foot of the cross and begged for mercy was cured. Others also claimed to have seen the good father himself and were also cured of any ills. Richard Coward White immortalized this shining cross in poetic form in 1882. The poem was published in the book *The Cross of Monterey & Other Poems* by Richard Coward (White San Francisco The California Publishing Company, 1882).

By The Cross of Monterey

"And the Indians told the Padre
That Portala's cross at night,
Gleaming with a wondrous splendor,
Than the noon-sun was more bright,
And its mighty arms extended
East and westward, O so far!
And its topmost point seemed resting
Northward on the polar star.
And they told, when fear had vanished,
How they gathered all around,"

Mission San Carlos Borromeo, Carmel, California.

The Mission Bells ~ Carmel

Ghostly Snapshot

Reports of bells ringing by unseen hands at both the mission and at the Presidio have surfaced. Once a group passing by the Presidio chapel heard the bells but upon further inspection found no one there to ring them. The bells at Carmel were said to ring spontaneously, as if calling the people to mass. Below is a poem from *The Bells of Capistrano and added Romances* by S. H. M. Byers (Potter Brothers Company Los Angeles, California, 1918).

"Still, at times they say it rings there,
Moonlight nights the most of all;
When a child has died they say it
Rings from yonder ruined wall.
And the land folks think that angels
Passing ring the mission bell,
And they cross themselves and whisper
When they feel the midnight spell."

Location

San Carlos Borromeo de Carmel Mission at 3080 Rio Road.

The Mission is open daily from 9:30am until 4:30pm (7:30pm June 1 to Labor Day) and 10:30am until 4:30pm Sunday. It is closed on Thanksgiving and Christmas Day.

The phone number for the gift shop is (831) 624-3600 or (831) 624-1271.

The website is www.carmelmission.org

"Now it is the time of night That the graves, all gaping wide, Every one lets forth his sprite..."
~ William Shakespeare, A Midsummer Night's Dream

El Camino Real ~ Monterey & Carmel

History

Gambling dens and houses of ill repute, driven by law from Monterey, found hiding places amid windings of the road to Carmel. By the late 1800s the gamblers need no longer hide on El Camino Real; they plied their trade freely and openly in Monterey. Before that time, when laws were strictly enforced, the road to Carmel was not one that you traveled alone and certainly not after dark. "Here Mexicans and Indians and Gringos gathered to gamble and revel and murder, till folk said Satan haunted that highway and were loath to travel by night," writes Grace MacFarland in her *History of Monterey,* published in 1914.

Manifestations

Reports are not limited to the early 1900s. Drivers today report seeing the image of a woman slowly materializing on the road, a phantom rider, the sound of a wagon that never appears, and even the sound of a horse neighing when there are none to be

Vintage collectible postcard, c. 1940s, of El Camino Real, HWY 101, California. Made by Stanley A. Piltz Company, San Francisco, California.

seen. Sightings on this road are so numerous that even the most skeptical must admit that this road is haunted.

"At first they tried to laugh it off as a mere figment of their imagination. But laughing had no effect on the ghost. He appears not to be sensitive to ridicule. He remained as mysterious, as weird, as uncanny as ever."

~ Author unknown, 1906

Point Pinos Lighthouse ~ Pacific Grove

Ghostly Snapshot

Emily Fish is still hard at work keeping the light at Point Pinos. She picks up after people and moves unsightly objects around. You might catch a glimpse of her if you visit the lighthouse. Of course Mrs. Fish is not looking her best these days, as she has faded with time, which isn't surprising as she was the light keeper at Point Pinos from 1893-1914.

Vintage collectible linen postcard of Point Pinos Lighthouse. You can see in this view the landscaped lawns and white picket fence of the light keeper's home. Made by Curteich-Chicago. On the back is "...*[sic]* is open to picnic parties and the entire community is interwoven with drives of exceptional beauty."

Point Pinos Lighthouse

Point Pinos was named by the Spanish explorer Sebastien Vizcaino in 1602. Before the lighthouse was built, Point Pinos was a treacherous place to navigate with many a ship's hull smashed against the rocks and the crews washed up onto the rocky shore. It was noted in the *Oakland Tribune* in 1914 that the booming of the waves seemed to "sing a dirge for the brave seamen who have met their death in the treacherous waters around Point Pinos."

The Point Pinos lighthouse, built in 1855, is the oldest operating lighthouse along the California Coast. Mr. Charles Layton's tenure was cut short when he was killed in the pursuit and subsequent arrest of Anatascio Garcia. His wife, Charlotte, then Allen Luce, and finally Emily Fish – who still seems to be checking in on the place, followed Charles Layton as keepers of the light.

Mrs. Fish

Work – some people love their work and others hate it. And still a select few can never imagine doing anything else but work, even after death. And so is the case with the ghost of the Point Pinos Lighthouse, Mrs. Emily A. Fish. She was born in Michigan in 1843 and later came to the West Coast after her marriage to a Berkeley physician, Melancton W. Fish.

Most female lighthouse keepers kept the positions after their husbands' deaths. Emily Fish won the Point Pinos position when her son-in-law informed her of the vacancy. This would be only one of many unique things about Emily Fish's tenure. In short order she moved herself, her luxurious furnishings, a Chinese servant called Lew Kew, and even set about landscaping the property. She was a hard person to work for, going through countless male employees whom she dismissed for incompetence. In her twenty-one years as lighthouse keeper, Mrs. Fish dismissed thirty men. Her station was considered one of the best maintained until her retirement at the age of seventy-one when she moved to a home on Sinex Avenue in Pacific Grove.

Manifestations

Mrs. Fish does not seem to realize her skills are no longer needed or that the lighthouse itself was automated in 1973. Her ghostly activities at the lighthouse primarily are confined to moving objects. If you put an item down on a table, for example, don't expect it to be there when you go back to retrieve it. It seems Mrs. Fish likes to clean up after everyone. Occasionally visitors have seen a blurry figure of a lady in Victorian dress. This may be a little surprising, but Kew Lew, who served Mrs. Fish even in retirement, has not returned with his mistress.

Location

Point Pinos Lighthouse is located on Asilomar Avenue between Del Monte Blvd. and Lighthouse Avenue, Pacific Grove.

Phone: (831) 648-5716

Hours of operation vary so it is best to phone ahead.

The website is www.pgmuseum.org

"In the past year, especially, inhabitants of the air or the streams or the graves of the many dead that lie buried all about the village have been wandering about like a colony of reckless night owls."

Author unknown, news report from 1904

Stokes Adobe ~ Monterey

Ghostly Snapshot

All old houses have their secrets. But only a special few, like Stokes Adobe dating back over one hundred and seventy-five years, have ghostly secrets. On the outside it looks normal enough—well kept with an inviting entrance. But there are at least two spirits in this home and a list of bizarre events.

Gallatins

When the Gallatins opened up a restaurant in the1950s on Hartnell and Madison Streets, they were fully aware they were buying a piece of history. Their new place of business was one of the most historic buildings in Monterey. Originally built as a single room adobe in 1833 by Benjamin Day, it was sold a mere four years later in 1837 to James Stokes.

James Stokes was one of the most colorful characters in Monterey history. It is said that he is one of the two spirits that still

Stokes Adobe, Monterey, California.

reside at the adobe. His diverse resume might read something like this: sailor-druggist-occasional doctor ... and mayor. He certainly knew how to move up the social ladder in Monterey. Marriage to a rich widow was one stepping-stone that eventually led this itinerant sailor to become the mayor of Monterey.

James Stokes started as a steward on board a ship that docked in Monterey. According to General John Bidwell, who wrote of this time in his book *Life in California Before the Gold Discovery,* James Stokes brought ashore "one of those little medicine chests that were usually taken to sea, with apothecary scales, and a pamphlet giving a short synopsis of diseases and a table of weights and medicines, so that almost anybody could administer relief to sick soldiers." It would seem the people of Monterey were under no illusion as to the extent of his medical training. In fact, he is highly praised by another important historical figure, Walter Colton, "Here is James Stokes, from England, for twenty-five years a citizen of Monterey, a merchant, farmer, and doctor, married to a lady of the country, in whom the afflicted always find a friend."

The lady Walter Colton mentioned was a wealthy widow by the name of Josefa Soto de Cano, widowed with four children. After their marriage in 1840, they had two more children. James expanded the adobe into a seven-room two-story house with a wing for the kitchen and storage rooms. *An interesting piece of California history is the housing of California's first newspaper press in one of the buildings on the property.

Over time the building changed hands and even saw life as a bakery under Honoree Escolle. Later, it was turned into a private residence again for Mortimer Gragg and his wife "Hattie," who purchased it in 1890. The Graggs were well known in the community and the home was said to be the site of many social functions right up until Hattie's death in 1948. Later the home was converted into a restaurant. The Gallatin Restaurant ran from 1950 until 1980 and various similar enterprises followed.

Manifestations

At the time of the writing of this book, the building was for sale. The then owners of the restaurant, Kirk and Dorthea Probasco, were quite proud of their ghost, devoting menu space to the stories. According to them, ghost stories dating back to the Gallatin's Restaurant period reported a figure of a man dressed in 1800s style clothing. It was assumed this was the ghost of James Stokes. Employees also saw the apparition of a beautiful woman, believed to be Josefa.

Many think the ghost of Hattie Gragg also haunts the building. Hattie Gragg loved to entertain and was a popular figure in Monterey. She lived at the building until her death and maybe this explains her continuing presence there. According to her great-great grandson, the former mayor of Pacific Grove in a *Monterey Herald* article by Marie Vasari said "...*[sic]* it was his grandmother, fond of a well-told tale, who started telling ghostly yarns about the place." He goes on to say the famous guests such as "Steinbeck and other artists and writers frequently gathered for meals at the Gragg home, where Hattie and Steinbeck would entertain each other with stories."

Could it be these stories so captivated the public imagination that over time they were perceived as fact? Maybe, but does this explain the sightings outside of the dwelling of a mysterious woman dressed in period clothing, of unusual cold spots in the garden, or ghostly encounters during the renovation process by construction workers?

Unusual happenings at the building have been recorded in the Monterey Peninsula over the years. One of the spirits at the house is mischievous, tapping guests on the shoulder. People sitting in the chairs on the left side of the main room will sometimes complain that someone keeps moving their chair. In one of the booths cold spots can sometimes be felt and on the staircase a ghost in period costume can be seen. Unusual occurrences are not limited to the downstairs either. Upstairs the mirrors in the main bedroom get nudged to the side and people have reported a disembodied female voice.

A former partner in the previous restaurant, Kara Caswell, was interviewed by author and psychic Atoinette May in *Haunted Houses of California: A Ghostly Guide.* She explained that the hauntings at the adobe could be broken down into two types. "One kind involved ghosts that people saw, the other involved things that happened." She listed many odd occurrences, ranging from untrustworthy employees caught in the act by spirits being scared off by those ghosts, to the sighting of a woman in a period black gown and the unmistakable sound of a rustling dress when no one was around.

Is the Stokes Adobe Still Haunted?

In the same *Monterey Herald* article by Marie Vasari, the former mayor of Pacific Grove dismissed any suggestion that the home was haunted, saying, "...*[sic]* he never experienced anything of a paranormal nature."

Whether the spirits of James Stokes and Hattie Gragg still dine at the adobe is left up to you. Hattie and James were certainly both attached to the building. Most people who have spent time at the adobe feel a presence – a guardian of sorts over the building. We shall have to see if the new owners of the building experience anything out of the ordinary. {20}

Location

The adobe is on the corner of Hartnell and Madison Streets. The property is currently for sale. Across the street is the headquarters of Ghost Walks of Old Monterey.

"Yet call not this long life; but think that I am, by being dead, immortal; can ghosts die?"

~ John Donne

Colton Hal ~ Monterey

Ghostly Snapshot

The Constitutional delegates meeting wrapped up over one hundred and sixty years ago but a few people seem to have stayed behind. Who could they be? Props at the table recreating the famed signing move and even more mysterious are the sounds of footsteps on the outer porch.

History

On July 7, 1846, Commodore John D. Sloat announced at Monterey's Custom House, "Henceforth California will be a portion of the United States." Three years later at Colton Hall, delegates met to design California's constitution. In 1850 California would become a state.

That moment in time is forever immortalized at Colton Hall, which operates today as a museum. Entry from the rear of the building takes you up a flight of steps into a small room where a staff member is always present. This section also houses a selection of books on Monterey and memorabilia connected

Colton Hall, Monterey, California. The hall was constructed in the 1840s.

Colton Hall, Monterey, California.

with the hall. The adjacent large meeting room is set to look as it did when the constitutional delegates met. The long wooden tables hold writing quills, inkwells, and drafts of the half-written constitution.

Manifestations

In this large main room listen for the mysterious sounds some workers have heard. Footsteps across the barren wood floors are frequently reported. When the guide looks up from her desk there is inevitably no one there or no one visible. One evening as a staff member was locking up, she heard someone out in the meeting room. She was certain no one had entered through the side entrance and the front had been locked up for over an hour. Getting up from her desk she cautiously approached the room. Though she had worked at the building for some time, something felt out of place that evening. As she entered the room, an odd sensation passed over her. It was as if the temperature in the room had suddenly plummeted. Looking down the length of the room she was both relieved and puzzled to see it was deserted. There were no open doors or any other sources of draft to explain what had happened. The footsteps she heard could have been echoes from the time the building had been converted into a hospital during the flu epidemic of 1918.

The Portico

Other ghostly activity at Colton Hall involves what is outside. A door in the center of the main hall opens out onto a large, square balcony with two sets of staircases on each side. It is something of local lore hangings occurred on this very spot, but this is not historically documented. It is assumed the spirits of those men and the convict labor used to construct Colton Hall still linger. As recently as 2002, *The Monterey County Weekly* printed a short story on hauntings in which they wrote, "According to local lore, some of the delegates never left. Others say that the ghosts are the spirits of three men who were hanged outside the building long, long ago."

Rumors

How did these rumors begin? Well, like any rumor, the origin is hard to trace but it is interesting to note as early as 1914 the balcony's "other" use was reported as fact in the following book, *Monterey, Cradle of California's Romance: the story of a lost port that was found again and a dream that came true*, by Grace MacFarland (Press of Weybret-Lee Co. Monterey, 1914). Ms. MacFarland wrote, "*Sometimes a man was arrested for a murder committed in a drunken quarrel and, especially if he were a half-breed Indian and the victim a Gringo, he was hanged with little ceremony to the portico of Colton Hall. The public school met in the old quartel in those days. Once it happened that a man was to be hanged at recess. All the children scampered over to Colton Hall to see the fun. Not till the criminal was safely dangling did the principal call them back to their studies, though the recess period was long past.*"

The children she mentions would not have had to "scamper" far as the lower portion of Colton Hall was the location of the public school. The author gives no source for her information but as she is writing of a period a mere fifty years earlier one is left to wonder if maybe there is some truth in her account.

Location

It is located on Pacific Street, between Madison and Jefferson Streets.

The museum is open 10:00 to 4:00 Monday through Sunday.

Thanksgiving, Christmas, and New Years Day it is closed.

Phone ahead at 831-646-5648

"Strange and weird noises were heard, the calling and groaning of the spirits of the dead miners...made the place hideous, ..."

~ Author unknown, newspaper report 1901

Steinbeck's House ~ Salinas

Ghostly Snapshot

On Central Avenue in Salinas is a grand Victorian built in 1897, once the home of John Steinbeck. Visitors on some tours these days get a little more than they expect when John Steinbeck's mother greets them on the staircase. This is amazing, since the woman in question died in this home in 1934.

History

After the death of his mother in 1934, John Steinbeck wrote to a friend that he felt the Salinas home was haunted. He also said he saw things walking at night in his childhood home.

Could the reports of a shadowy figure of a woman on the narrow staircase be Steinbeck's mother. One lady on a summer tour received the fright of her life. After getting off her tour bus she took lots of snaps of the sign—Steinbeck House restaurant and gift shop. Ghosts were the last things on her mind. She was interested in hearing about Steinbeck's early life and writing.

Manifestations

After lunch, the group was taken on a tour. The lady began to have the odd sensation she was being watched. She put this down to many hours on a bus and being surrounded by the authentic

Steinbeck furniture. Of course it was easy to imagine the great writer still residing at the home. As her group walked towards the staircase, she looked up to see the specter of a woman wearing a rather old fashioned dress. Thinking the woman was part of the Steinbeck tour, she smiled at her, waiting for the woman to come down the stairs so the group could make its way up. The woman instead simply vanished.

Besides the phantom image of Mrs. Steinbeck, the author himself has been seen on the lower level.

Location

132 Central Avenue
Salinas, CA 93901
(831) 424-2735
www.steinbeckhouse.com
For information on hours & tours see the website

"A ghost is someone who hasn't made it – in other words, who is dead, and they don't know they're dead. So they keep walking around and thinking that you're inhabiting their – let's say, their domain."

~ Sylvia Browne

The Royal Presidio Chapel & Rectory ~ Monterey

Ghostly Snapshot

In life the padre tended to his congregation and in death he still returns for mass, to light the candles and to offer comfort to parishioners. Such are the tales from the Presidio chapel and Carmel Mission. A loyal dog looking for his master in the afterlife in the courtyard of one building or chasing after him though the owner is nowhere to be seen. A neophyte makes his way across the Mission grounds at dusk. Why would a padre, a spectral dog, and a neophyte haunt the Royal Presidio Chapel and the Carmel Mission? If there is any substance to these stories, maybe the answers lie in the years just before their deaths.

The Royal Presidio Chapel & Rectory, Monterey, California.

History

Formerly known as the San Carlos Cathedral, the Royal Presidio chapel was built in 1770. Father Junipero Serra founded it on June 3, 1770. It is not only the first Californian cathedral but the oldest operating church in the state. A Mission next to a military establishment was seen as a deterrent to attracting neophytes who might view the military as a threatening presence, so Father Serra decided to move his mission to the present day location in Carmel. The chapel in Monterey continued to serve the local population, providing spiritual guidance to the soldiers of the Presidio.

To visit the chapel is truly to step back in time. It is California's first cathedral and oldest continually functioning church. A worn sandstone façade decorated with carvings greets the visitor with two large bells dominating the upper left hand side of the church. The niche high above the front entrance once held the first non-indigenous sculpture in California, Our Lady of Guadalupe. When she was taken down for restoration residents of Monterey, parishioners, and even a mariachi band were in attendance. Currently the entire building is undergoing renovations in an effort to preserve this historic building. Cypress trees, which graced the grounds, were found to be destabilizing the building. One docent told me "the roots were growing up in between the layers of plaster of the church." At the time of this writing, the church has been closed to visitors since 2007.

Manifestations

Legend has it the chapel is haunted by the ghost of a nineteenth century priest whose footsteps still echo in the sanctuary. Candles light up and burn when no one with access to the chapel admits to lighting them. These events were even recorded in the *Encyclopedia of California's Catholic Heritage, 1769-1999*.

One evening when a man was deep in study he heard an unusual sound by the door. There was something about the noise he couldn't quite place. Thinking it would go away he returned to his work but soon heard the sound again. The man got up from his desk, curious to see who was out in the hall. Looking down an empty corridor he saw a floating candle.

When the church closed for renovation in 2007, the Reverend Peter Crivello, pastor of the chapel, interestingly chose to quote Winston Churchill in his address to parishioners. He said, "We shape buildings and the buildings shape us." Perhaps the devotion of the parish and clergy to San Carlos past and present is as tightly woven into the structure as were the roots of the cypress trees which once graced its grounds.

The Royal Presidio Chapel & Rectory, Monterey, California.

Location

This building is located on the path of history at 550 Church Street. Walk past the charming church school and rectory building before the chapel. A great view of the bells and alcove where the Madonna stood is seen from across the street, the area where the Presidio used to stand. If the chapel is open, docents will kindly guide you through the building.

"Be silent in that solitude, Which is not loneliness – for then The spirits of the dead, who stood In life before thee, are again In death around thee.."

~ Edgar Allan Poe

6

Guests Who Won't Leave

Introduction

A place to rest your head, put your feet up, and relax after a busy day is what people are looking for in a hotel stay, but some of you reading this account wouldn't mind the odd visitor. No, not room service, but maybe a guest who also stayed in your room ... let's say one hundred years ago. OK, so maybe the bed rattling and the insistence on turning off the television at all the good parts or turning on the television just when you are about to doze off can get on your nerves, but this is why you are here – for the haunting.

Sleeping with a ghost may sound like a line from a movie but tales of spectral guests and haunted hotels are found throughout America. Many places openly discuss their haunted tales in magazines, books, and in other promotional materials. Even rooms with poltergeist activity are on occasion occupied ... but *nobody* sleeps in the infamous room on the Queen Mary, that famous luxury liner now dry-docked in Long Beach. There are not many guests tolerant of shaking beds and flying objects. Some establishments not wanting the publicity or perceived intrusive visitors trampling through lobbies with electromagnetic field recorders or thermal-imaging digital cameras prefer their "spirits" to be left in dark staircases and dusty wine cellars.

The Hotel Del Monte ~ Pacific Grove

Ghostly Snapshot

Luxury hotels with their private gardens, first class dining, and beautiful accommodations are meant to pamper guests.

The Hotel Del Monte vintage collectible postcard, cancelled 1913, Carmel, California. This view shows the main entrance of the hotel.

The Hotel Del Monte did such a good job that even in death guests never want to leave. Content to stroll gardens, sit at their favorite table, and occasional wreck havoc, the hotel stopped operating long ago but the guest register is still open.

History

Welcome to Monterey's most haunted hotel; this historic building is one of the most modern and elegantly appointed hotels on the Pacific Coast. It is an imposing white structure with a red tile roof, one hundred and twenty feet, a Spanish style tower on the main building and a huge two hundred foot dining room. Upstairs, as was the custom in grand old hotels, is a large ballroom, used presently as a banquet room. Hidden passageways are said to wind around the building's old walls.

The hotel was established in 1880 by four tycoons. The Pacific Improvement Company acquired seven thousand plus acres of land on the peninsula. The luxury resort was an outlet for a new branch line connecting Castroville and Monterey. Almost instantly it became the destination of choice with its distinctive European hospitality. One hundred and twenty-six acres of private landscaped gardens, two hundred trees, shrubs and flowers, tennis courts, and a fifteen-acre lake surrounded the hotel. And the hotel had its very own railroad station. The hotel attracted the rich and famous and was a coveted destination for sixty-two years. At its peak, the Hotel Del Monte hosted 17,000 visitors yearly. This was almost eight times the population of Monterey!

The Hotel Del Monte was the spot to stay on the West Coast, attracting socialites, movie stars, and presidents. Travels to the Del Monte made newspaper headlines and your name was sure to appear in a list in the society column with the rich and famous. Sadly, the hotel burned to the ground in 1887 and the "Grande Dame of America" was reduced to ashes. The fire chief of the original 1887 hotel is said to still haunt the building but there have been no recorded sightings. This fire was but one of several fires to damage the hotel. Was this due to bad luck, arson or a supernatural explanation? The hotel was not closed for long. It was rebuilt in an astounding hundred days. The Del Monte was back in business with a guest book equally as sparkling. If you peeked into the hotel registry, names such as Benjamin Harrison, Teddy Roosevelt, President McKinney, Charlie Chaplin, Gloria Swanson, Clark Gable, and even Salvador Dali are written there.

The Curse

In April 1900 a small fire would damage the clubhouse at Del Monte – but the bowling alleys and wine cellars were saved thanks to an alert night watchman. It was around this time that dark rumors made their way into regional papers. Was the Del Monte cursed the reader was asked? One reporter, "A strange feature of the disaster is that none of the rare shrubs and plants that surround the clubhouse and render it one of the most notable spots in the Del Monte grounds were injured in the least." Fire would strike again in 1924. The hotel was rebuilt in 1927 but with the depression and World Wars the resort fell on hard times. In the 1950s, the Defense Institute bought the hotel and the Naval Academy Postgraduate School moved here from Annapolis. With no major fires at the site since it changed hands maybe the perceived curse had more to do with building standards then to anything supernatural.

The Hauntings

Phantoms

Phantoms at the Del Monte were long present. Hotel staff not only engaged in ghost talk, but was in fact encouraged in it according to one reporter from *The San Francisco Call* in 1907. He first noted with curiosity many couples strolling in a particular section of the grounds during the early evening hours. Thinking this was the Del Monte's designated "lovers lane," he made inquires and was rewarded with what he called a "summer ghost" story. Without a "lovers leap," he explained to his readership, the hotel concocted its own tale of star-crossed lovers.

The Phantom Rancher ~ Pacific Grove

At one time, a large ranch stood on the Del Monte land. The daughter of the ranchero, Maria, longed to be a part of life in the town of Monterey. Since her mother died, her father had forbidden her to go into town. Fearing the day she would also leave, he kept her under strict surveillance. One morning, a local fisherman set up his nets near the ranch. Maria became friends with the boy. As friendship deepened into love, Maria knew her father would not approve of this poor fisherman. After months of secretly meeting by the shore, the young lovers were discovered. In a rage, Maria's father locked her in the ranch house.

The fisherman tried to persuade the rancher to let him marry Maria but he was firmly rebuked. The old rancher threatened to kill the fisherman if he ever set foot on his land again. One evening, the fisherman attempted to free Maria. As he crept around the home, the rancher surprised him and crushed his skull with an abalone shell. Maria's heart and spirit were crushed by her father's cruel act just as surely as her lover's skull and she died soon after in deep and terrible grief. However, in another version, young love triumphs as the fisherman prevails and it is Maria's father who is bludgeoned to death with an abalone shell!

What to Tell the Guests?

Hotel guests were told they could spot the ghosts of the rancher, Maria or the fisherman if they wandered the lawn of the

Hotel Del Monte in the early evening. Though the reporter claimed never to have seen a thing, "Guests claimed that they could see the ghost of the old rancher plowing by moonlight, hammering his shadowy steed with a spectral lath in a field back of the stables." As for recent sightings, there haven't been any recorded; then again, with the site now being a military installation, looking for spectral farmers probably ranks low on their "to do" list.

The Man in Grey ~ Pacific Grove

The lights are dim. The crowd buzzes with excitement. The first notes float through the air and another glamorous evening at the Del Monte begins. The ballroom is full of dancers and the sound of rustling gowns can be heard in the former lobby. One man is seated at his favorite table near the bandstand. He enjoys his drink and takes in the dancers as they whirl by. He would invite you to sit but invitations to this event went out one hundred years ago.

Sightings of "the man in grey" are numerous. He sometimes appears in the hotel's lift, on staircases, in the lobby, and in the large ballroom. One theory is that it is Charles Crocker who died at the hotel August 14, 1888, at the age of sixty-six. Charles Crocker was a large man and the ghost most people report seeing is a trim man with a grey beard wearing a suit. Local papers and magazines have tried to find out. One reporter from *Coastal Magazine* in 2003 invited Carmel Valley psychic Patrick McAnaney to visit the grounds.

It was the psychic's first visit to the academy. Upon entering the ballroom he picked up the presence of a man. He is reported as saying, "This place might actually have a ghost..." *[sic]* "He scampers around. He's an older man. He had stomach cancer—he knew he was going to die. He was very wealthy, and cranky because he couldn't eat what he wanted. I think he's here, which is really, really unusual. He cheated a lot of people and he's afraid to die."

One worker at the present day Naval Postgraduate School was standing in a corridor when she had a sensation of someone at her side. Turning quickly, she was in for an even greater shock. The corridor was empty. Which of the Del Monte's ghosts had paid the woman a visit is a mystery. Was it the Man in Grey, the best known of the former hotel's spirits? She certainly came into contact with someone or something.

Local Monterey historian and author Randolph Reinstedt has written extensively on this spirit after interviewing staff at the academy and guests to the dining room. He never saw anything, nor did the reporter in 2003, but the people they interviewed certainly did. These experiences range from lights flicking, objects moving, shoulder tappings, and an elevator operated from the inside stopping between floors with no one in it. A strange apparition has even been seen near the tower.

Some very psychic people have not only seen the man in grey, but also a woman dressed in evening wear.

The original hotel probably enjoyed the possibility of the presence of ghosts and encouraged the stories in order to titillate their many guests. The Naval Academy leaves the larks to the cadets!

Location

The Naval Academy is located at 1 University Circle. Visitors can visit the site by first checking in at the main entrance or the Quarterdeck. Brochures with a self-guided walking tour of the hotel grounds are available. The beautiful ballrooms and dining rooms still maintain their charm and elegance.

"All houses wherein men have lived and died are haunted houses. Through open doors the harmless phantoms on their errands glide, with feet that make no sound upon the floors."

~ Longfellow

Ghostly Chickens ~ Pacific Grove

Ghostly Snapshot

Spectral ships, cars, dogs, and now chickens? A very old legend on the peninsula concerns a ghostly hen and her chicks. It sounds like something suited to Saturday morning cartoons; but, as you know, appearances can be deceiving.

A Girl Called Kate

A girl never identified by the newspapers, but I shall call Kate, was traveling from San Francisco to the Hotel Del Monte

Not so ghostly resident in the Larkin Garden, Monterey, California.

for a weekend getaway. Motor trips along the coastal highway were a popular excursion for city dwellers at the turn of the twentieth century just as they are now. Special columns in the *San Francisco Call* entitled "Toot Toot," or in later years "Automobile," extolled the virtues of driving, and one popular drive regularly featured was the trip to the Del Monte.

The friends entertained each other on the long trip by telling stories. After several hours the party reached Monterey and checked into their hotel. They met for dinner in the formal dining room of the Del Monte and the cheerful banter and stories continued. Over dinner one friend recalled a tale that took place a few miles from the hotel.

As told to Kate, during the late 1700s, when Father Serra was at the Mission San Carlos Borromeo de Carmel, another priest met with a terrible end. He was taking some chickens to a neighbor when a thief attacked the priest and stole the chickens. When the thief checked the sack, the chickens were gone. Confused, he returned to the spot where he left the priest. The chickens were busy pecking in the blood soaked dirt around the padre's body. The thief quickly stuffed the chickens in the sack again. A few meters down the road he realized the sack was again empty. It is then he realized he had cursed himself. Distraught, the man, whose head was suddenly filled with the deafening sound of chickens, killed himself.

In some versions the priest awakes with a bad headache and in other versions he is dead. What is consistent in the stories is that the chickens and hen are never found. They only appear at the same spot in the road. To see them is a premonition of your death.

Kate was interested in the story and asked many questions. After dinner the group went for a drive along 17-Mile Drive. To Kate, who was at the wheel, it must have seemed later as the sun was setting and deep in the forest the canopy obscured the light. As the party neared the ghostly spot, a passenger in the car, trying to be humorous, yelled that he could see the chickens on the road. Panic struck, Kate lost control of the vehicle and the car veered off the road, slamming into a tree trunk.

At first it appeared luck was on their side. The group was able to walk away from the accident. Kate was taken back to the Del Monte Hotel and treated by the hotel doctor. Kate was in shock and the doctor was called in to "clear her (Kate's) mind of chickens."

Kate was never quite right again. I failed to mention that the waiter warned Kate after everyone else had left the dining room. If you ever see the hen and her chicks, you won't lose your life but you will lose your mind. The staff at the hotel saw Kate's incident as validation that there is some truth in folktales. {21}

Manifestations

The sound of a hen and her chicks or the sudden appearance of them is a warning of danger. There are no reports of any recent sightings but the superstitious believe in the early evening hours that ill-fated spectral hen and her brood wander the Carmel area. No one has ever caught them on camera, but maybe you will.

Location

Though the grounds of the hotel are off limits, you can go for a drive along 17-Mile Drive, one of only nine private toll roads in the United States. When the hotel first opened, carriages would take guests on this gravel road around the Peninsula and through the Del Monte Forest.

"It is, alas, chiefly the evil emotions that are able to leave their photographs on surrounding scenes and objects and who ever heard of a place haunted by a noble deed, or of beautiful and lovely ghosts revisiting the glimpses of the moon?"

~ Algernon Blackwood

La Playa ~ Carmel

Ghostly Snapshot

A girl dressed in a wool bathing suit heads down to the shore. Swimming hasn't been allowed at this point for years due to the rough ocean conditions but fearlessly she wades into the deep water and disappears. Don't bother to search for a lifeguard; this girl went for that swim in 1909.

History

La Playa was originally built in 1905 by the Norwegian artist Christopher Jorgensen, as a private residence for his bride, Angela Ghirardelli of the famous San Francisco chocolate manufacturing family. Christopher Jorgensen is best known for his paintings of California missions and Yosemite National Park. He attended the San Francisco Art School (California School of Fine Arts) where he later became an instructor and then administrator. It was here he met his future wife, Angela Ghiradelli.

By 1906, the Jorgensens left Carmel and leased their former home to Agnes "Alice" Signor. La Playa remained in the Signor family for many years. The Cope family of San Francisco bought the hotel in 1983 and extensively renovated the property in keeping with its Spanish themed architecture.

Vintage collectible postcard of La Playa Hotel, Carmel, California, with a view of the interior gardens.

Today the hotel is one of only fourteen properties in California designated a Historic Hotel of America by the National Trust for Historic Preservation. It is an elegant, charming hotel, a popular destination for visitors.

A Girl Alone With Her Thoughts

Mrs. Signor, keeper of the bathing pavilion, swept out the sand from the changing stalls. Before long the beach would be crowded. The beach was the major attraction for visitors from San Francisco and locals, August being the high season. Pausing, Mrs. Signor glanced up at the striking figure of a young lady as she passed by the deck chairs. The girl pushed her brown hair under her bathing cap, ignoring the other early risers who had staked claim to a piece of sand. The girl was alone as she had been every morning for the past few weeks. Finding this odd, Mrs. Signor had made a few inquiries in the village. She had been told this was Alida Ghirardelli, daughter of Domingo Ghirardelli, founder of the famous San Francisco chocolate factory. Alida was also the niece of the artists Mr. & Mrs. Jorgensen whose home was the site of many artistic gatherings. The girl was staying by herself as her Aunt and Uncle were away at another home in Yosemite. It soon became obvious to locals that Miss Ghirardelli was quite at home with her own company. When residents of Carmel would be asked to describe the girl in the weeks to follow they would comment, "She (Alida) was a girl who preferred quiet solitude to society."

Alida established this morning swim ritual soon after her arrival and so it was this warm August morning where we find Alida. After what had occurred only two days previous, Mrs. Signor felt compelled to keep an eye on the girl. Only two days previous, she had nearly drowned in the surf. She watched as Alida swam out into choppy waters, her tanned arms slicing through the white caped surf. Mrs. Signor muttered to her dog about "foolish headstrong girls," but soon her thoughts were occupied elsewhere. With the sun well up, she was busy attending to her customers. The pavilion was the central meeting place for families, couples, and the resort community.

It was a child who first heard the screams. All eyes turned to the ocean to see two arms flailing in the water. The crowd watched in horror as Alida was hit by wave after wave, unable to break free from the surf. Perhaps inspired by a legendry Carmel story in which a large Newfoundland dog was credited with saving a child from drowning, Mrs. Signor ordered her collie dog into the waters. As the dog raced to the shoreline a second dog lunged at it and a fight ensued. Two men raced to the Pine Inn, a good distance from the Carmel River for a boat. Frantically they dragged the boat along the sand but by the time they launched it, Alida had slipped from view. In published reports, one of these men dove into the water and nearly drowned but was pulled to safety. Bystanders reported that they knew it was too late before the men even launched the boat.

Rumors

After Alida's death, rumors of suicide circulated. One was a report recorded in the *San Francisco Call*, which stated only two days before she died, Alida had a near drowning experience at the same spot. According to witnesses on the beach she appeared reckless and often swam out too far. She alarmed others on the beach such as Mrs. F.B. Signor who trained her collie dog to swim after the girl, fearing the accident that ultimately took place. Why did Alida repeat her foolish behavior?

Newspaper reports speculated on her motives, insisting she swam out for a long distance with deliberate intention of losing her life. Tabloid headlines littered San Francisco papers – "Tragic End Witnessed By Scores" – "Noted Heiress and Social Favorite Loses Life While Swimming in Ocean" – "Throngs Helpless As Girl Cries For Aid / Two Men Narrowly Escape Death in Vain Attempt to Rescue Drowning Woman" – "Rumors of Suicide Scouted By Friends" are some examples.

To her family these rumors were hurtful and preposterous. Alida, they said, was an independent, beautiful, and wealthy girl. Why they asked then would she take her own life? The Ghirardelli family insisted there were no failed love affairs or "hidden sorrow" as one reporter wrote. Alida was a good swimmer who enjoyed her early morning swims. It was not unusual for her to be alone with a sketchbook as she was an accomplished artist. Alida studied at the Mark Hopkins Art Institute and in Europe where, according to Sidney Lawrence in the article "The Ghirardelli Story," she was influenced by the Impressionist painter Mary Cassatt.

Local Japanese divers were hired by the Ghirardelli's to recover Alida's body, which was presumed entangled. One month later her body was recovered, not by these divers but instead by a local resident, J.W. Hand, of The Carmel Development Company, in Carmel River. The body was taken to Watsonville where the medical examiner on September 12, 1909, hoping to squash all rumors of suicide, listed the cause of death as "accidental drowning." Alida was twenty-seven years old when she died. {22, 23}

Manifestations

Sightings of Alida, both on the beach and at the former home of her Aunt and Uncle, now the La Playa Hotel & Cottages, began after her death and continue today. Is Alida still "alone with her sketchbook and her thoughts," wandering along the shoreline?

One early morning, a woman walking along the beach, watched people playing with their dogs but one figure near the shoreline stood out. It was a girl with brown hair attired in an old-fashioned swimsuit. Before she could approach the figure, the girl disappeared, "swallowed by the mist."

Guests and staff at La Playa Hotel & Cottages have seen the apparition of a dark haired woman. There is some disagreement as to the identity of this person. History would indicate Alida but some people believe Angela is still caring for the home she once loved. Over the years, a ghostly female image has appeared on the stairs, in the lobby, and in the gardens. "The legend changes like the wind, ...," says longtime La Playa Hotel Concierge Julie Dillon. According to Dillon (whose interview you can see on the Historic Hotels of America site), "Carmel residents like to believe the rumor that Angela drowned in Carmel Bay and her ghost haunts the shores of Carmel's white sand beach." We know of course it was not Angela but Alida. Dillon is also quoted as saying, "I believe that when someone passes away, their soul often returns to the place they loved the best."

*Story Note—Alida's name was consistently spelt wrong in local papers, sometimes appearing as Alita. Alida Ghirardelli was born in 1881 and died in 1909.

Location

Camino Real at 8th Ave
Carmel, CA 93921
Phone (831) 624-6476
Driving directions are available from the hotels website at laplayahotel.com

It is a short walk from the village of Carmel or a short drive from Monterey. Carmel River State Beach is a mile-long beach known for its bird sanctuary. Swimming is not allowed on Carmel Beach due to the rough conditions and violent undertow. Located conveniently off Highway 1, one mile south of Ocean Avenue. Directions are available on the California State Parks website.

"What terrified me will terrify others; and I need only describe the spectre which has haunted my midnight pillow."
~ Mary Wollstonecraft Shelley

Haunted Ranch House ~ Carmel Valley

Ghostly Snapshot

A peaceful ranch house on the outskirts of Carmel is home to a spirit trapped by a horrific event.

History

When Frederick Preston Search and his wife, Opal, moved from their Orinda, California, home in 1949 to a three hundred acre ranch house near Jamesburg, in Carmel Valley, they never expected it to be "occupied." The Searchs were composers. He was a cellist with the Oakland Symphony, formerly with the Boston Symphony. Rosalind Sharpe, in the *Pine Cone Cymbal* and later in the Oakland papers, first profiled their very haunted home in Carmel.

Frederick and Opal Search active in the musical world bought a ranch in the Carmel Valley. They moved from Orinda with a truckload of belongings. These belongings included seven cats, ducks, a turkey, and an Irish Setter. The pastoral location of Carmel Valley was suited to their lifestyle more than an urban center. The home they found was a rundown ranch house. The old Tularcitos adobe section of the house was the original grant house and estimated to have stood for more than one hundred and ten years. The exact history was unknown and it was this history that would come back to haunt the Searchs. The ranch had a wooden staircase with worn steps that rose from the kitchen on the main floor to a second level.

A staircase in the heart of Carmel, California.

Manifestations

Over the years, a number of people connected with the ranch house, including "*[sic]* ... the occupants, as well as valley old-timers, saw the ghost descending the staircase." Speculation in the area gave this descending ghost as the reason why so many had moved away from the house. The ghost was said to be that of a young Indian girl. According to Ben Bloomquist, who was recorded as being "a valley old-timer" and who lived at the ranch house as a handyman "*[sic]* the ghost has been seen by many reliable people and dates back to Spanish days when a young Indian girl lived in one of the upstairs rooms of the adobe part of the house."

Exactly who this girl was we do not know but according to Ben's story, two men had fallen in love with her. It is thought she accepted one and rejected the other's affections. This rejection so angered the man he broke into the home and murdered the girl while she lay sleeping. Since this tragic occurrence, the form of a beautiful young girl began appearing on the upper level of the home.

The girl was always dressed in a chemise or nightgown and seen at the top of the stairway. Over the years, she had startled more than one visitor to the home. The owners, alone in the building, heard the distinct sound of someone walking on the stairs. These sounds were not the "creakings" or "groanings" of an old home but the unmistakable sound of a person descending the stairs.

It was noted the ghost methodically walked the upper level as if she was familiar with the home. The phantom never spoke to anyone, nor was there any poltergeist activity. There was only the "clear sound of feet on the wooden boards." Though the paranormal activity was confined to the upper level and the staircase, Mr. Bloomquist did tell the reporter he had heard the ghost in the kitchen.

As unnerving as this was, the Searchs made no mention of moving. They went ahead with plans to renovate their home. The old staircase where the ghost had been most active was taken down, not because of the haunting but due to modifications made to the house's design. The girl and the phantom footsteps were never reported again. {24}

What Causes an Apparition?

From 1908 comes this explanation of what causes a non-physical image or an apparition, *"Apparitions at the spot where some crime was committed are usually thought forms projected by the criminal, who, whether living or dead, is perpetually thinking of the circumstances of his action."*

~ AHT 1908

Background

Frederick Preston Search was known as a cellist, conductor, and composer. During his long and extremely interesting life he performed around the world, earning a reputation as a talented instrumentalist. Some of his local Carmel connections include his direction of the orchestra at the Del Monte, supervising the orchestra and choir at the Monterey High School, and serving as president of the Musical Arts Club on the Peninsula. Selections of his works are available at The Music Library, 240 Morrison Hall, University of California, Berkley.

"The murdered do haunt their murders, I believe. I know that ghosts have wandered on earth. Be with me always—take any form—drive me mad! Only do not leave me in this abyss, where I cannot find you!"

~ Emily Bronte, Wuthering Heights.

7

Classics

The Pearls of Loreto ~ Monterey Bay

"We attended a gala event at the theater with the most beautiful ladies of Mexico," boasted the Empress Carlota in one of her letters, "who arrived covered in pearls from the Gulf of Cortez [sic] and dressed in the latest fashions from Paris."

Ghostly Snapshot

Along the cliffs on Monterey Bay watch out for two fleeing figures. The first one will have pearls wrapped around her neck and the second will be bleeding profusely from a wound he suffered hundreds of years before. Meet the favorite of Monterey, Ysabel Herrera, whose beauty inspired one man to murder.

Pearls in California?

Rumors of gold, pearls, and other undiscovered deposits of wealth were rampant in Europe after Christopher Columbus returned to Europe. According to author C.S. Mayo of *Miraculous Air: Journey of a Thousand Miles through Baja California, the other Mexico*, "Beginning in the sixteenth century, pearl fishers from the mainland crossed the Sea of Cortes to work the rich beds around the Bahia Peninsula. Pearls from the Bahia de la Paz were used in coronets, scepters, and in clothing."

There is a legend born of this time called "The Pearls of Loreto." The mission of Our Lady of Loreto is located in the town of the same name, established on October 25, 1697, by an Italian Jesuit Juan Maria de Salvatierra. The mission was named for the Lady of Loreto and was the first of the California missions. The Madonna statue was reportedly covered in pearls, which ended up wound around the neck of a lady from Monterey.

La Favorita

The most wonderful collection of pearls anywhere in the world was collected by the Indian divers of the Loreto Mission. Year after year they harvested the pearls for the Fathers of the mission. These pearls were not for sale, but for decorating the statue of Our Lady, the Blessed Virgin, in the monastery at Loreto in Lower or Baja, California.

When word reached the other missions of this great project, every pearl brought up from the waters of Monterey or anywhere else along the coast of California was taken by the Indians to the padres. Pearl after pearl was placed on the statue of Our Lady of Loreto.

Not everyone was happy that the pearls were given. One woman called Isabel Herrera craved these pearls. They filled her every thought as she vowed one day to make them her own. In some stories Isabel appears as a poor beauty, therefore oddly justifying her greed, and in others no reason other than desire is given.

One day Isabella tells her suitors if they want to prove their love for her then they should bring her the pearls of Loreto. No one seems very shocked by this, perhaps equating the unattainable pearls with the equally unattainable heart of Isabel Herrera. One boy decides to win Isabel's heart and rides night and day until he reaches the church. Rushing inside he grabs the pearls off the statue and murders the priest who tries to stop him. Seemingly unaffected by his crimes, the boy rides back to Monterey, pearls in hand.

The boy presents the pearls to Isabel and the two appear at a grand party that evening. Isabel, glorious in her pearls, basks in the admiration of the crowd. The moment is short-lived, as a padre from the Loreto Mission rushes into the room and accuses the boy of theft and murder.

The guilty pair flee for the bay, hoping to reach a ship that is about to sail, but they never make it. As they skirt the cliff, shots ring out, killing the boy. Isabel then leaps into the bay. Neither she nor the pearls are ever recovered.

Small Madonna statue.

In one of my favorite versions, Isabel develops super human strength (tongue in cheek) and lifts up her beloved in her arms, then leaps off the cliff. In yet another version, the story is set around Thanksgiving with the boy being an Americano who robs the Lady of Loreto on this day. This is given as a reason why Thanksgiving is not a time to celebrate in Monterey!

Manifestations

On foggy days, look for the image of a young woman dressed in a floor length gown wanders by the bay. She seems to be searching for something. As you approach this odd figure, she fades into the fog. This ghostly woman has company. In addition, a Spanish soldier quickly walking across the grass has been seen. He disappears just as quickly, seemingly as if a door has simply opened and closed on the spot.

Location

Monterey Bay plunges as much as 6000 feet – perhaps it is no wonder the pearls have never been found! It is twenty-five miles across the mouth of the Bay from Lighthouse Point, Santa Cruz to Point Pinos in Pacific Grove. If you don't plan to plunge into Monterey Bay, try a sight seeing cruise from the wharf.

"For who can wonder that man should feel a vague belief in tales of disembodied spirits wandering through those places which they once dearly affected, when he himself, scarcely less separated from his old world than they, is for ever lingering upon past emotions and bygone times, and hovering, the ghost of his former self, about the places and people that warmed his heart of old?"

~ Charles Dickens, Master Humphrey's Clock

The Lost Silver Mine ~ Monterey Peninsula

Ghostly Snapshot

Did the priests who came to the Monterey area have hidden silver mines? Stories abound in Monterey papers from the 1800s up until the present with reports of lost treasure found. Due to the nature of Monterey as a vibrant port and the rough seas it is normal that silver pieces and other artifacts are found. Many of these silver pieces have Italian markings, obviously not from lost mines.

The Legend

According to legend, the mine was discovered soon after the Jesuits founded their settlement at Carmel. It is impossible to say whether knowledge of it was gained first by priests or by Indians. Some accounts say the Indians knew about it long before the priests came and others say it was stumbled upon accidentally when the builders of the mission were seeking suitable rocks for construction. The priests did not go into the mountains for the silver, only the Indians went out and brought back the precious ore at night. Wherever the silver was hidden, it took three days for the Indians to return with it. There were some at the Mission who thought this was merely a trick and the mine was not far at all.

Ghostly Snippet

An Englishman journeying through the town of Monterey chanced to see some of the silver from the padre's mine. He quickly organized a group of men who spent several weeks exploring the surrounding countryside but they could find no trace of the mine. The Englishman's ragtag group deserted him for better pickings elsewhere but he vowed to never give up. To this day the Englishman is said to be still searching for the padres' silver. {25, 26}

Manifestations

Deserted mineshafts throughout the peninsula usually have at least one ghost tale connected to them. Voices and cries of trapped miners are the most popular stories, which leads to the question – Are spectral miners still hoping to strike it rich?

Mystery Carmel Mine May Be Long Lost Mine of Padres

"The Lost Mine Found!" was on the lips of many residents back in the 1940s. A newspaper published a report stating the padres' silver had been found in Carmel. This was an incredible find to be sure—sadly, it wasn't true.

The loss of several lambs and cave-ins on Mission Ranch Club land led one local resident to believe treasure was close at hand. The shafts were said to be "*[sic]* ...extending in a straight line 50 feet apart from the Carmel Mission in line with the holes at a ranch house occupied by Muriel Vanderbilt..." The mine was never found, but several silver pieces did turn up. Sadly, they had Italian markings on them! The reason for the tunnel leading from the mission to the ranch is still unknown, but at the end of the tunnel is a ghost. Yet another white lady ghost lurks in the bunkhouse of Mission Ranch. This white specter appears in a loose white gown, hovering a few feet above the ground. It is not known who she could be or whom she has been waiting for all these years.

The Revolt

In the long list of possible reasons why no mine has ever been found comes this one from *The Pasadena Union* on October 29, 1887. This article stated the Indians erased all trace of the gold mine when they revolted against the padres. There are two obvious things wrong with this story. The first being, the complex history of the Missions in California is very well documented and nowhere is it written the Indians at the Carmel Mission revolted. Secondly, the padre's fabled mine was a silver mine and not a gold mine.

The Secret

In this story two rival Indians hold the secret of the lost mine. The men's feud began as they pursued the same girl, who didn't marry either. She was the only wise person in the story!

As their hatred grew, one of the men decided to reveal the location of the mine to an Americano prospector for a large sum of money. Why would he reveal the location and not dig for the silver himself, you may wonder? It was said that both men were much too lazy to dig for it.

The man set out to mark the trail to the mine, unaware that his rival was following him. The two rivals met near the mouth of the mine and what happened next is not known but the old prospector never received his map. As for the two rivals, their bodies were never found.

Manifestations

The spectral images of an Indian is said to wander in the vicinity of the mine. This angry spirit shows himself to anyone who foolishly gets too close to the mine. If, when camping on the peninsula, you are awoken around midnight, cautiously look behind you. You might see a pair of angry eyes looking back.

"Darkness—darkness—no pain—nothing but darkness; but I am passing on and on through the darkness: my thought stays in the darkness, but always with a sense of moving forward."

~ George Elliot (Mary Anne Evans)

8

Day Trips

Haunted Hearst Castle ~ San Simeon

Ghostly Snapshot

Why does a ghost care about housekeeping? That's the question facing the staff at our next haunted location.

History

Build it up and tear it down, no these weren't the actions of an exuberant grade-schooler tackling his first building project, but of William Randolph Hearst. It was not uncommon for him to change his mind and order a grander replacement. The Neptune Pool for example was rebuilt three times. It is little wonder that the estate was never fully completed. Though it is now called Hearst Castle, this name was detested by Randolph Hearst, who called it La Cuesta Encantada – "The Enchanted Hill," or alternatively "the ranch house." The estate is so large it cannot be viewed in one day. First time visitors to Hearst Castle are amazed to find they must choose between four different daytime routes, not including the specialty tours. It is little wonder that guides must go through over one hundred hours of training.

Work on the home lasted for twenty-eight years and costs are estimated at $40 to $100 million. The art for the home was collected between the two world wars. Today you would never be able to accomplish this feat again without spending reaching into the stratosphere. If you are unable to make a visit, see the website (address given below) for an overview of his staggering collection.

Hearst Castle was donated to the State of California in 1957 by the Hearst Corporation. It is one of the most popular places to visit in the California State Parks System. It has been fascinating people long before tour buses began climbing up its long drive.

People began talking about Hearst Castle since construction began in 1919. Reports of his guests playing with baby elephants or feeding giraffes and the legendary and glamorous guest list, which included Charlie Chaplin or Winston Churchill, sparked public interest.

"William once had a circus party where all the guests dressed as clowns, jugglers, and lion tamers. He even brought in a merry-go-round," writes Barbara Knox in *Hearst Castle: An American Palace*. Who wouldn't want an invitation to Hearst Castle?

William's father, George Hearst, bought the estate near San Simeon in 1865. A ranch once stood on the grounds that the castle occupies. Julia Morgan, a well-known San Francisco architect, was responsible for the castle, working closely with William Hearst over many years to realize his dream – a dream that would never see completion in his lifetime. Buildings were put up and taken down as Hearst continuously revised the project. The book *Hearst Castle: An Interpretive History of W.R. Headrest's San Simeon Estate* by Nancy E. Loe devotes one section to this working partnership.

Haunting

Reports of a haunting at the Hearst Castle surfaced in the 1960s. One haunting made news in *The Fresno Bee* in 1963. The reporter did a quick survey of the fifty-five permanent employees. The majority of guides interviewed said the castle was haunted! Was it William Randolph Hearst coming back to his beloved home or perhaps one of the famous guests?

One bedroom in the castle was the scene of many unusual disturbances. A moving rug was one of the most unnerving disturbances reported by guides. Not Ali Baba and the flying carpet but a rug that was moved around the room by unseen hands. As soon as it had been straightened out, the guides would find it curled up by one of the bedposts.

The rug in question looked like one of the hundreds of imported rugs covering most of the floors in the rooms of the castle. It was located in a bedroom in the south tower, a part of the castle not visited by tourists. Leaving the room in perfect order, bewildered guides would return to find the rug curled up against one of the bedposts. "No one goes in there, except the staff. None of us will admit, at least, to curling up a corner of the rug, so how does it get disarranged?" said an unnamed guide. "We straighten it out, then the next time someone enters the room, the rug is out of place," another guide was quoted as saying.

Guides spoke of an eerie sensation standing in the room. Sudden cold spots and the feeling of an unseen presence brushing up against them were experienced. "The hairs on the back of the neck seem to prickle, almost as though the same ghostly hand that plays games with the rug is tugging away playfully," said the unidentified guide. {27}

Recent Sightings

No recent reports of paranormal activity have surfaced, but a child visiting the castle is said to have seen a figure peering out from Mr. Hearst's bedroom. It is thought this was the spirit of the famous man himself. If you are able to tour the castle you might pick up some vibrations from the past. Better yet, gaze up into the windows ... you never know who will be looking back.

Location

Hearst Castle is located at 750 Hearst Castle Road in San Simeon, California.

Please see www.hearstcastle.org for complete driving directions and visitor hours.

"All houses are haunted. All persons are haunted. Throngs of spirits follow us everywhere. We are never alone."

~ Barney Sarecky

The Point Sur Lighthouse ~ Big Sur

Ghostly Snapshot

While walking the property of the Point Sur Lighthouse, "breathtaking" is the word that comes to mind. The booming and crashing of waves and the 1889 lighthouse rising out of the point fills your senses. Another word that applies is "haunted"—just ask the phantom light keeper.

History

A procession of cars line up for today's tour of the Point Sur Lighthouse. After winding their way to the base of the rock, visitors must say goodbye to transport and hike another quarter of a mile to the lighthouse. By the time they have reached the base, a sense of the solitary life early light keepers had is well understood ... or is it? To truly understand the remote location, visitors should imagine climbing up a staircase of 395 steps, which was formerly the only way to reach the light.

Constructed in 1889, the Point Sur Lighthouse is not only a California Landmark but a protected landmark on the National Register of Historic Places. Lighthouse keepers and their families lived here until 1974. Reports of hauntings and unexplainable events at the lighthouse go back to its beginnings. When standing near the light it is hard to imagine any human activity having an impact or even being a match for the natural forces around, but the hauntings at the light have become as much a part of the landscape as the howling wind and crashing waves.

Manifestations

The Point Sur Lighthouse is an even eerier place at night, when spectral sailors from past wrecks sometimes appear on the bluff. Only on a moonless night can you see the fog-like images slowly taking shape. You might be temped to think it is safer in the tower, but another ghost or two are here. One is known for a distinctive cough. Docents at the light have heard on occasion the sound of coughing when no one is around. This audible imprint from the past is thought to be the child of a keeper who succumbed to TB.

Unexplainable noises including banging and footsteps, the feeling of being watched, and unusual cold spots are all other paranormal occurrences at the light. A few people claimed to have seen an image out of the corner of their eye. This blurry image dressed in a light keeper's outfit disappears the instant you turn to look for it. In the *Monterey County Weekly*, docents at the lighthouse spoke of a phantom who liked to work the cash register, causing it to spew tape. They also mentioned the old beacon rotating by itself in the fog-signal room. Very creepy indeed....

Still haunted?

Definitely! The spirits of the Point Sur Lighthouse are as restless as the water around it. No wonder it is known as the 4th most haunted lighthouse in America.

Location

The Point Sur Lighthouse is located nineteen miles south of Carmel on Highway 1.

For information on daylight and evening tours and hours of operation, please see the website at www.pointsur.org

Phone (408) 625-4419.

"At last it came — a soft, irregular sound of footfalls on the stairs! They were slow, hesitant, uncertain, as of something that did not see its way; to my disordered reason all the more terrifying for that, as the approach of some blind and mindless malevolence to which is no appeal."

~ Ambrose Pierce

The Winchester Mystery House ~ San Jose

Ghostly Snapshot

Sarah Winchester may have died on September 5, 1922, but some say her spirits never left her house. Organ music, lights mysteriously turning on, bulbs bursting, snippets of conversation heard in "'empty' corridors," and even misty apparitions all point to a home that is very much occupied. Isn't this fitting for a home built for the spirits?

Sarah Pardee Winchester

At the advice of a medium, Sarah P. Winchester moved out West after her husband's death. William Winchester, the son of the famed Winchester rifle manufacturer, left his widow Sarah more than forty million dollars. Money would bring Sarah Winchester no

Collectible postcard of the Winchester Mystery House, Santa Cruz, California. Stanley A. Piltz Company, San Francisco, California. On the back is written, "The three million dollar Wonder House, built as the spirits directed...".

happiness. Her husbands' death, combined with the death of her only child, impacted Sarah's mental health. Little is written of her mental instability in the East but by the time she had established herself in Santa Cruz there is little doubt she was in a fragile state. This instability would manifest itself in her odd architectural demands and her self imposed isolation.

The widow arriving in San Jose in 1884 was not in her right mind. Sarah built a home for herself and the spirits of a select crowd among the departed, convinced that the spirits of the people killed by the Winchester Rifle were haunting her. This was not just any home mind you, but one that would forever keep growing and changing to accommodate the new spirits harmed by the rifle.

The home had its own heating, lighting, water, and sewer system. Many of its features are considered modern and desirable today. It is estimated that she poured $5 million into her building project, which was never finished. The home included 1,000 windows, gold and silver chandeliers, art glass windows, and doors inlaid with German silver. It is estimated she spent more than $500,000 at Tiffany's alone. When she bought material, she purchased the entire bolt so nobody could duplicate the pattern. After her death, enough fabric was found for a store, bolts costing hundreds of dollars had small pieces missing the size of a handkerchief. When the 1906-earthquake hit, she believed it was the result of excessive spending on her part, so she ordered thirty-one rooms boarded up.

When Sarah died she left the home to a niece, who removed the furniture. This took over six weeks to accomplish. The home was turned into a museum in 1923, with guided tours. This would be the first time the home was open to the living as Sarah turned away famous guests such as Theodore Roosevelt.

Manifestations

Today, one hundred and sixty rooms still stand of an estimated seven hundred and fifty chambers interconnected by trick doors, self-intersecting balconies, and dead-end stairways. Famous psychics and guides have all experienced strange phenomena at the home. Organ music is the most common of these occurrences, as Sarah played music to entertain the spirits. Sarah Paradee has also been seen in various rooms in the house. As for the spirits of the people killed by the Winchester rifle, none of them have ever been seen.

Location

525 South Winchester Boulevard
San Jose, California 95128
(408) 247-2101
Hours- 9:00 am – 5:00 PM /June to Sept. open to 7:00 pm
Be certain to check the website regarding tour times.
www.winchestermysteryhouse.com/

"Unfortunately, our feelings do not always respect the law of probabilities, and to me that evening, the possible and the impossible were equally disquieting."

~ Ambrose Bierce

The Jinx Ship ~ Point Sur

There was once a jinx ship used as a barge between Oakland and San Diego. During a very heavy storm off Point Sur, the man on watch saw a tall figure in oilskins on the forecastle. "He wore a slicker and sou'wester hat, glistening from the wet," said the man. The figure strode back and forth, then disappeared. Minutes later the man on watch was astonished when the mate appeared beside him. The mate denied ever being forward on the boat. So who was the man in oilskins?

The mysterious man in the slicker would often appear during storms, only to disappear before unsuspecting crewmembers. It was never determined who the ghost could be, but the ship became so feared amongst sailors that her owners found it difficult to find crews brave enough to sail on her. {28}

"Now a haunted ship is even less desirable than a haunted house, because when the spooks, be they real or fanciful, go on a rampage, the ship is harder to abandon."

~ Syl Macdowell

The Phantom Locomotive ~ Santa Cruz

"The dog is the greatest friend of man no doubt about that, as he is endowed with the power of seeing ghosts, devils and death. When you hear your dog howling it is a proof that he is warning you against some evil event."

~ Mexican superstition, author unknown, June 23, 1907

Ghostly Snapshot

Eyewitness reports of a mysterious train riding the rails near Santa Cruz are mentioned in old coastal papers. It would have retired from service around the turn of the twentieth century but this phantom train is still running on schedule.

The Light

Haunted cars, phantom ships, and now trains are the stuff of horror movies. One well-known locomotive on the San Francisco to Monterey run was not the kind you waited for by the tracks. You could not buy a ticket, nor would it show up on the train boards, although conductors on the route knew her well.

Conductor Billy Crawford credited the phantom with saving his life. One evening he was traveling to Santa Cruz with two men from Vermont. He was trying to impress them when he became

Haunted train tracks?

aware of a strange light on the other track coming, not from on the road in front of him, but from behind." "The light came from a locomotive which was tearing along behind him on the parallel track." "...contrary to all railroad rhyme or reason, it was running inbound on the outbound track."

Billy and the foreman both saw it and turned pale. "It was almost as if the force of gravity were suddenly reversed. But it was there, sure enough, and drawing steadily nearer." Already the headlight was abreast of the rear coach of Crawford's train. It crept silently-silently, there was the terror of it – on and on, gaining, gaining, until at last it flashed beside them, neck and neck." This sounds like something out of a an early Steven Spielberg film starring Dennis Weaver as the mild-mannered traveling salesman who is hunted down by a semi-truck and its driver.

Crawford continued on his route keeping one eye on the track in front of him, while nervously looking over at the other locomotive, which at times seemed to be passing him. According to news reports, "suddenly it came over Crawford that there was no locomotive of honest iron and steel. It was diaphanous." He could look through it and beyond, and catch the quick shadow of the telegraph poles as they hurried by – catch, too, the gleam of passing lights, right through the bulk of its boiler. There was no one in the cab – neither fireman nor engineer – to guide its headlong flight.

Old timers at the railroad yard had told him stories of this train, but he never believed until now. More importantly he remembered her appearance always occurred at a time of danger. He applied the air brakes without delay, and as his train slowed down and stopped, the phantom vanished. Swinging to the ground he ran ahead and there, just in the outer gleam of his headlight, a huge automobile lay overturned upon the track, its frightened occupants crawling from the wreckage. Billy silently thanked the phantom locomotive.

There have been no recent sightings of this train, but if you asked Billy, he would tell you that she was still riding the rails into eternity. {29}

Manifestations

The ghost train is rarely spotted these days. Some say if you walk along the abandoned sections near Los Gatos Creeks you might hear it as it moves up and down the line.

Location

The South Pacific Rail Company abandoned their mountain route in 1940 after a severe storm. The route along Los Gatos Creek is now part of a hiking and bike path. If you like steam trains, then hop aboard the c. 1890 train at Roaring Camp, in Felton. The train travels through Henry Cowell Redwoods State Park on its way to the Santa Cruz Beach Boardwalk. The trip takes about three hours and is well worth it. See the official site at www.roaringcamp.com

"For my own part, I never saw a ghost except once in a dream. I feared it in my sleep; I awoke trembling, and lights and the speech of others could hardly dissipate my fear."

~ Mary Shelley

The Phantom Rider ~ Morro Bay

Ghostly Snapshot

Some people become very attached to their homes, belongings, and even daily routine. Here is one ghost who is the life of the party in death.

History

Tales of phantom riders are not lacking on the peninsula. Around the Carmel Mission there are stories of a mystery rider on a white steed, always galloping south. Further down the coast are stories of a mystery steed always galloping up in the direction of Monterey. Here is a tale of Don Canet, a grand house, and the fiestas that seem to continue among the ruins.

Along the coast route between LA and San Fran is Morro Castle, built in 1831 by Don Vincent Canet. Who was Vicente (Cane) Canet? Don Canet sailed from Spain in 1824 aboard the *Asia*. He jumped ship at Monterey in 1825 and soon found himself married to beautiful and wealthy Rosa Maira Josefa Buitron y Dominguez. They wed in Monterey in 1828. He stayed for twelve years at the Presidio and was granted Rancho San Bernardo in San Luis Obispo County. He achieved prominence as the administrator and juez (a judge) of the Mission San Luis Obispo.

Vintage postcard, c. 1940, of Morro Rock, California. Made by E.C. Kropp Company, Milwaukee, Wisconsin.

The landmark castle lies a short distance from Morro Rock in San Luis Obispo County, just outside of the mission town. Don Canet used skilled Indian labor from the missions of San Luis de Tolosa and San Miguel the archangel. The main hall was eighty feet long. He spent over $40,000 for labor and materials, which was more than two hundred feet long with wings extending on each side to form three sides of a court with walls three feet thick. It was plastered with crushed gypsum from the nearby hills and the flooring was brought around the horn in sailing vessels.

Don Canet lived in grandeur – "Many a fiesta, many a bear and bullfight, many a wild horse broke the monotony of life if monotony could ever be in a land so fair and favored." After his death the castle was sold.

Manifestations

After Don Canet's death, rumors began of hearing his steed chomping and neighing in the courtyard at night. Townspeople swore they heard unusual sounds from the castle, and shadows seemed to take human form. There were a few sightings of a man and woman in Old Spanish dress descending one of the staircases. Don Canet himself was spotted riding his steed down to the water.

The reason given for Don Carnet's restless spirit is that his friends disobeyed his last wish, which was to place his body atop Morro Rock. This is why Don Canet is still seen galloping down to the bay and sometimes rowing a skiff towards the Morro Rock. As you drive down to Big Sur along the coastal highway don't be surprised if you see a white steed and rider dressed in finery of yesteryear. It's just Don Canet on his way to a fandango in Ol' Monterey. {30}

Legend

A wreathlike cloud, which forms above Morro Rock, is also attributed to the restless spirit of Don Canet.

Location

The picturesque town of Morro Bay is located halfway between Los Angeles and San Francisco.

See the official Chamber of Commerce site for directions. www.morrobay.org

Juan Rodriguez Cabrillo named the area during an expedition in 1542. You cannot climb Morro Rock as many of the stones are loose, thus making climbing hazardous, but you can visit the base of the rock.

"If such appearances (apparitions) take place, it still seems to me absurd and disproportionate to suppose that they do so in order to warn us, or help us, or hinder us, or anything of the kind. They appear for their own unfathomable reasons."

~ The Four-Fingered Hand Barry Pain

The Bispin Mansion ~ Capitola

Ghostly Snapshot

If the stories are true, the ghosts of a nun and an unidentified lady are frequent visitors to this newly restored mansion. The images were frequently seen amongst the ruins.

History

Once upon a time a beautiful mansion overlooked the town of Capitola. The mansion built in 1921 by Henry Allen Rispin and his wife, an oil heiress, Annette Winfeld Blake. Mr. Rispin owned most of the land in the immediate area of Capitola. He was planning on selling off lots to people from San Francisco as cottage retreats. His own mansion was part residential home and part "sales" office.

In 1929, before the Rispins could enjoy their home, they lost their fortune and were forced to sell to millionaire Robert Hayes Smith. He was to share the same fate as the Rispins, declaring bankruptcy in 1936. His Capitola holdings were liquidated, including of course the mansion. For the next few years the mansion remained empty until the Order of The Poor Clares purchased the home for their St. Joseph Monastery.

When the Poor Clares moved to Aptos in 1959, investors acquired the estate and in the 1960s a caretaker lived in a residence on the property, but squatters and even a hippy commune moved in. Sadly, the property was vandalized and many myths began to circulate of phantoms on the property. The Rispin mansion being newly renovated by current owners have been asked about phantoms but they laugh, saying visitors expect a ghost but there isn't one.

Manifestations

When the mansion was abandoned, there were sightings of a phantom nun. The woman dressed in long, grayish brown habit appeared barefoot, walking by the building. It is thought to be the apparition of one of the Poor Clares. It has never been determined if one of the sisters died here. Even if the current owners have no need of a ghost, they couldn't do better than a nun. Who better to watch over the security of the guests?

Location

The Rispin Hotel in Capitola, 2000 Wharf Road, Capitola, CA
Website at rispinhotel.com

For information on the Poor Clares, see www.poorclaresofaptos.org

"The phenomenon (ghost photography) is so mysterious, so miraculous, that even after the fullest evidential investigation I find it difficult to yield to conviction. I cannot say in what these materializations consist; I am only ready to maintain that there is something profoundly mysterious that will change from top to bottom our ideas on nature and life."

~ Dr. Charles Richet, member of the French Academy, photographer of ghosts. April 1906

The Mystery Spot ~ Santa Cruz

Vintage collectible photo postcard of the Santa Cruz Mystery Spot. Maker unknown.

The world has gone topsy-turvy, or at least the Mystery Spot in the redwoods of the Santa Cruz Mountains. The Mystery Spot has been entertaining people since it was first discovered in the 1940s. Park your car and pay the five-dollar admission charge. This 150-foot diameter area is billed as an area where the laws of gravity have gone haywire.

You walk at a seventy-degree angle up a winding path to a small cabin positioned at a sharp angle. As you approach the spot the lean becomes more acute as you proceed towards the center.

What's Inside

Inside this house, balls roll-uphill, chairs sit on walls and people lean over so far they can't see their shoes, yet they don't fall down. Your guide asks one person to stand on a level block then someone else on another level block. For some reason one person is higher than the other but on the block they are the same size.

Vintage collectible photo postcard of the Santa Cruz Mystery Spot.

Maker unknown.

In the shack on a hill, the guide then gets out an old board and places a ball on it. The board is diagonal but the ball rolls upward instead of down. You walk sideways not on your own accord but because you have to and when you are outside the shack you are still standing diagonally.

Vintage collectible photo postcard of the Santa Cruz Mystery Spot. Maker unknown.

A Scientific Conundrum

When you visit the spot you might be told a meteor of some kind fell near the Mystery Spot, a UFO is buried there, or a combination of mystical forces have created this place. Or if you are traveling with a couple of Professors from the University of Berkley they will probably utter something about vertical and horizontal cues and optical illusions. Have fun and don't think about it too hard.

Location

The Mystery Spot is found at 1953 Branciforte Drive.
The mailing address is Box 2817, Santa Cruz, CA 95063.
The telephone number is 831-424-8897

"We know so little what nature comprehends – what are powers and limits – that we can scarcely speak of anything that happens as beyond it or above it."

~ Thomas Street Millington

The Brookdale Lodge ~ Santa Cruz

Ghostly Snapshot

Marilyn Monroe and President Herbert Hoover don't dine here anymore, but eighty-seven spectral guests just couldn't leave the famed dining room. Ever since the 1900s, the lodge has been a popular destination due to the unique dining room.

The Lodge

More than one hundred years ago Judge James H. Logan built the Brookdale Lodge. The Judge is better known as the creator of the Loganberry. The lodge consists of forty-six motel rooms and two cottages nestled under the redwoods. The lodge sits between Boulder Creek and Ben Lomond on Highway 9. A Dr. F. K. Camp was the next owner of Brookdale Lodge and he had many creative architectural ideas.

A 1920s collectible postcard of the Brookdale Lodge showing the famous stream running through the dining room. Made by Curt Teich & Company, Inc., Chicago, USA. On the back of the card is written, "In the heart of the Big Tree country. Come linger with us and listen to the sound of the brook singing merrily through our dining room."

The most radical of these ideas was expressed in the dining room in the 1920s. The entire room was designed around several trees and a flowing brook, the idea being that you could catch your own dinner! Today, it would be illegal to do this, but in the '20s this was considered genius marketing. Dr. Camp is quoted as saying "*[sic]* the interesting part of watching the fish there (the brook) each year is they always return to the same rock they hid under the year before." Perhaps, he meant, if they managed to escape the frying pan!

The lodge began to fade in the 1940s and 1950s, becoming a gangster hangout. It was during this time that bodies buried under floorboards and other wild rumors garnered more attention than the stream.

The Brookdale Lodge, once called "America's Most Unique Hostelry," is still in operation and, though you can't catch your own fish anymore, a ghost may be included on the menu.

Manifestations

A young blond girl dripping wet appears at your table. She is gone before you can summon a waiter or scan the room for her parents. This is the ghost of Dr. Camp's niece, Sara. Sara drowned in the dining room creek. Sara is not alone, her mother is said to keep her company. This ghost's presence is signaled by the scent of magnolia. Interestingly, there have never been any documented sightings of the man who began it all, Dr. Camp.

Check It Out

Make sure you visit the "Mermaid Room," a small room whose only window looks into the bottom of the lodge's pool.

Location

11570 Highway 9
Brookdale, Santa Cruz 95007
831-338-6433
www.brookdalelodge.com

"Do you believe in ghosts? Nonsense? Not a bit of it? That merely shows that you have never seen one, but it doesn't prove in the least that there are none."

~ Gertrude V. Gabbs writing in 1906

9

Mini Investigations

If you would like to explore some of the more interesting sights right in the heart of Monterey, check out the following locations.

Lara~Soto Adobe

Giant Sequoia tree in front of the Lara-Soto Adobe, Monterey, California.

Under the large cypress on the front lawn is said to be the grave of an infant. There are no known sightings at the home but orbs and sudden temperature fluctuations have been noted. John Steinbeck, who only resided at the home for a year in 1944, is said to have had it exorcised before moving in.

Location: 460 Pierce St.

Underwood~Brown Adobe

The home was used by Jose Maria Sanchez, a wealthy rancher, when he was in the town of Monterey. Sanchez was rumored to have buried a treasure of gold dust and coins he earned gambling near his home. After he drowned in the Pajaro River, the search for his "treasure" began. Some believed his wife was cursed, as after his death she would marry four more times. Each of these husbands also met with an untimely death.

Location: next to Colton Hall.

Capitola Theatre

The theatre is said to be haunted by several spirits. These include dead patrons of the theatre who can be heard talking occasionally in the theatre. There is also the ghost of a past owner.

Location: 120 Monterey Avenue

Casa Munras

Casa Munras is said to house the apparition of a man, possibly Don Esteban Munras, dressed in a suit from the 1800s. Other paranormal activity at the hotel includes mysterious fog-like shapes and orbs.

Location: 700 Munras Avenue

The upper balcony of Pacific House. The building was constructed in 1847.

Pacific House

Bull fights and bear wrestling were held in what is now called "Memory Garden." As the sun sets, listen for the sounds of disembodied voices.

A well in a garden along the Path of History, Monterey, California.

The Perry-Downer House, Monterey, California. Manuel Perry constructed the home in 1860. Does one of the former occupants still reside there?

Perry~Downer House

Look up into the lace covered windows to see the spirit of a lady gazing down on the street below.

Location: 201 Van Buren Street

Top Ten Places To Find A Ghost

The following information is provided by author and ghost investigator, Fiona Broome and appears in her book, *Ghosts of Austin, Texas.* For more information, visit http://hollowhill.com/.

No matter where you are, certain locations are usually haunted. These sites don't always have ghosts, but they're the best places to start when you're looking for unreported visitors from beyond the grave.

Theatres

Ghosts frequent places where people have performed on stage. These include movie theatres that were once performance halls.

There are three kinds of ghosts at these locations:

First, at least one actor who is still seen on or near the stage.

Second, a stagehand lingers backstage, usually around the lighting or the curtain controls.

Finally, someone appears towards the back of the hall, especially during rehearsals. He or she almost always smokes a cigarette that people can smell, or they'll see the smoke or the burning ember.

Battlegrounds

Almost every battleground has some residual energy from the violent and tragic deaths that occurred there. Some battlegrounds are actually haunted by the spirits of the men and women who died there, too. Between Texas' battles for independence, Indian attacks, and Civil War conflicts, you'll find many locations with ghost stories ... and real ghosts.

Cemeteries

It's a cliché but a true one: Ghosts haunt cemeteries. Modern graves—burials that occurred less than fifty years ago—are rarely haunted for very long.

For the most powerful hauntings, look for graves that are at least one hundred years old. Only a few are haunted, but you'll find elevated EMF levels at many of the graves, especially if they're unmarked.

Colleges

Almost every college or university reports at least one ghost. Most also report poltergeist phenomena. The performing arts center is often the most haunted location on campus. In Austin, the University of Texas campus is probably the most haunted college.

Summer Camps

Most camps—especially Scout camps—have a ghost or two. Usually, these are benevolent ghosts of former camp counselors or the camp manager. An aroma of perfume or pipe smoke is usually reported, related to someone who worked there.

Very Old, Large Homes and Buildings

Like most ancient castles, many very old, large buildings have ghosts. In an older home, a woman who lived there lingers to be sure that the house and its occupants remain safe. She usually wears a green dress.

Another ghost is mad and lurks in the attic, basement, or an outbuilding. A variation on this is a ghost in the nearby woods or a field next to an old homestead. These hauntings are almost predictable.

Old Hotels

Many hotels are haunted by the same people who visited them in life. They're usually happy ghosts who return to relax and enjoy themselves.

Classic haunted spots in hotels include the top floor, the elevator, and the lobby. This is true of the Driskill Hotel, Austin's most haunted and elegant hotel, and a favorite destination for visiting ghost hunters.

Around Austin, this category of haunting extends to former brothels. In the late nineteenth century, dozens of feisty, independent-minded madams owned "boarding houses" around downtown Austin. Today, these sites are often clubs, bars, and restaurants in the entertainment and warehouse districts of Austin. Most of them have great ghost stories to share.

Hospitals, Retirement Homes, Morgues, and Funeral Parlors

As you'd expect, some people aren't willing to leave the last place where they were seen and called by name. However, if these sites are still in use, they're usually off-limits to ghost hunters.

Instead, look for former locations of these kinds of buildings. They're usually haunted by perplexed and sometimes angry ghosts.

Around Austin, there are probably hundreds of unreported ghosts. If you follow these suggestions, you'll find even more ghosts than are included in these pages.

"While yet a boy I sought for ghosts, and sped Through many a listening chamber, cave and ruin And starlight wood, with fearful steps pursuing Hopes of high talk with the departed dead."

~ Author unknown

Your Own Ghost Stories

If you would like to share your own ghost stories send them to stories@anitayasuda.com

What to include:

Where the sighting occurred.

Number of people witnessing the event

Ages and or occupation of the people involved.

Date & Year

History of the building or area where said event occurred.

Describe the event as best as you can, including as many details as possible.

The garden behind the First Theatre, Monterey, California.

Selected Bibliography

Colton, Walter. *Three Years in California*. New York: A.S. Barnes & Co., 1850; Cincinnati: HW Derby & Co., 1850.

Davis, William Heath. *75 Years in California*. San Francisco: J. Howell, 1929.

Forbes, A.S.C. *Mission Tales in the Days of the Dons*. Chicago: A.C. McClurg & Co., 1909.

MacFarland, Grace. *Monterey, cradle of California's romance; the story of a lost port that was found again and a dream that came true.* Monterey: Press of Weybret-Lee Co., 1914.

Marinacci, Mark. *Mysterious California.* San Carlos, CA: Wide World Publishing, 1988.

Morrison, Frederick. "California Bell Legends: A Survey." In: *California Folklore Quarterly*. 1945. Vol. 4, No. 1, pp.27-28.

Reinstedt, Randll A. *Ghost Notes.* Carmel, CA: Ghost Town Publications, 1974.

Smith, Barbara. *Ghost Stories of California.* Renton, WA: Lone Pine Publishing, 2000.

Skinner, Charles M. *Myths and Legend of Our Own Land.* 1797.

Slevin, L.S. *Guide book to the Mission of San Carlos at Carmel and Monterey*. Carmel: Carmel News Co., 1912.

Weber, Francis, J. *Encyclopedia of California's Catholic Heritage, 1769-1999.* Mission Hills, California, and Spokane, Washington: St. Historical Society and The Arthur H. Clark Company, 2001.

Articles

1. Anon. "Christmas in California-La Gama del Pescadero." *Daily Alta,* December 25, 1858.

2. Anon. "Chinese Ghost." *Oelwein Register*, October 23, 1890.

3. Anon. "Haunted Cypress of Monterey." *The Standard*, July 11, 1903.

4. Anon. "Haunted Cypress." *The Washington Times,* July 12, 1903.

5. "California Sea Serpent Is Seen Again." *The San Antonio Light*, San Antonio, Texas, August 20, 1939.

6. Anon. "Looks Down The throat of 'Sea Monster'." *Amarillo News-Globe*, Amarillo, Texas, May 12, 1940.

7. Anon. " 'Old Man of Bay,' Weird Sea Monster." *Angler Nevada State Journal,* May 13, 1940.

8. Anon. "Sea Monster Reappears At Monterey." *The Hayward Daily Review*, September 18, 1941.

9. Anon. "Sea Monster Appears Again." Lowell, Massachusetts, October 19, 1950.

10. Knox, Jessie Juliet. "Sherman's Broken Promise." *Oakland Tribune Magazine*, July 16, 1923.

11. Costigan, A.B. "Romantic Legends of the Beautiful 17 Mile Drive at Monterey." *The Call*, June 27, 1909.

12. Anon. "The Return of Vasquez." *The New York Times*, May 4, 1876.

13. Cox, Dick. "Tiburcio Vasquez, Lover-Bandit." *Real West Magazine*, November 1965.

14. Gomez, Don Juan. "What I knew about Murieta and Vasquez." *The San Francisco Call*, October 14, 1900.

15. Propes, C.B. "Legend of the Fifth Joaquin." *Independent Press Telegram*, February 2, 1958.

16. Anon. "Anastasio Garcia." *The Monterey Sentinel*, November 17, 1855.

17. Anon. "Hanged by a Mob; The Murderer of a Woman Lynched; The Doomed Wretch Makes His Will Under the Fatal Tree." *San Francisco Chronicle*, March 17, 1873.

18. Tays, George. "First Theatre in California Berkeley." *California Historical Landmarks Series*, 1936.

19. Masters, Ryan. "Rootless Variety: The Homeless Troupers of The Gold Coast Keep on Performing." *Monterey County Weekly*, May 05, 2005.

20. Vasari, Marie. "Treasure For Sale." *Monterey County The Hearld*, December 26, 2007.

21. Anon. "Ghostly Chickens." *Oakland Tribune*, December 4, 1910.

22. Anon. "Alita Ghirardelli Sinks To Death in Surf Near Carmel." *San Francisco Call*, August 17, 1909.

23. Anon. "Alida Ghirardelli's Body is Recovered." *San Francisco Call,* September 12, 1909.

24. Anon. "Into a Haunted House The Ghost's Story." *Oakland Tribune*, March 30, 1947.

25. Shepardson, Lucia. "Who Sealed The Silver Monterey Padres?" *The San Francisco Call*, October 9, 1910.

26. Anon. "Mystery Carmel Mine May Be Long Lost Mine of Padres." *Times & Daily News Leader San Mateo*, March 11, 1940.

27. "Guides at Famed Hearst Castle Are Mystified By Moving Rug." *The Fresno Bee*, March 10, 1963.

28. Macdowell, Syl. "Unsolved Mysteries of the Sea." *Oakland Tribune*, September 7, 1929.

29. Cagy, F. Jay. "The Phantom Locomotive." *The San Francisco Call*, May 10, 1908.

30. Anon. "Legend, Tale of Phantom Rider." *The Fresno Bee*, June 18, 1939.

Index